IDIOM'S DELIGHT

IDIOM'S DELIGHT

Fascinating Phrases
and
Linguistic Eccentricities

Spanish ◆ French ◆ Italian ◆ Latin

SUZANNE BROCK

Illustrations by Laura Lou Levy

VINTAGE BOOKS
A DIVISION OF RANDOM HOUSE, INC.
NEW YORK

First Vintage Books Edition, December 1991

Copyright © 1988 by Suzanne Brock
Illustrations copyright © 1988 by Random House, Inc.

All rights reserved under International and Pan-American
Copyright Conventions. Published in the United States
by Vintage Books, a division of Random House,
Inc., New York, and simultaneously in Canada by
Random House of Canada Limited, Toronto.
Originally published in hardcover by Times Books,
a division of Random House, Inc., New York, in 1988.

Library of Congress Cataloging-in-Publication Data
Brock, Suzanne.
    Idiom's delight : fascinating phrases and linguistic
  eccentricities / Suzanne Brock ; illustrations by
  Laura Lou Levy. — 1st Vintage Books ed.
        p.   cm.
    ISBN 0-679-73410-4
      1. Romance languages—Figures of speech.
    2. Romance languages—Terms and phrases.
    3. Romance languages—Idioms.   I. Title.
  [PC255.B7   1991]
  440—dc20   90-55703
                    CIP

Book design by Naomi Osnos

Manufactured in the United States of America
10   9   8   7   6   5   4   3   2   1

For Janie and Pat

ACKNOWLEDGMENTS

I wish to thank Susan and Ralph Gross for their sage comments on the original manuscript. I'm deeply grateful to Maia Gregory, who suggested the form this book should take.

They have been at a great feast of languages,
and stolen the scraps.

> —Shakespeare, *Love's Labour's Lost*

. . . the root function of language is to control
the universe by describing it.

> —James Baldwin

CONTENTS

IDIOM'S DELIGHT

IN PURSUIT OF IDIOMS

Although we speak a grand, rambunctious language, we use the same idioms over and over until the imagery is lost. This book aims to remind you of the riches of your everyday speech, and to throw some light on the equivalent riches in other languages.

I've divided this book into four sections: Spanish, French, Italian, and Latin. Each of the foreign phrases has been paired off with a comparable phrase in American English. Well, that's not quite true. The Latin section is Odd Man Out, with some wonderful epigrams and idioms that have no counterpart in our language. So be it.

The end result is tidy, but I never thought it would be, for in the pursuit of idioms I wandered off in all directions, sometimes getting lost for days. Delving into words is a haphazard, self-indulgent pastime. Once you give in to its pleasures, here's what can happen.

Browsing through a book of proverbs, you come across the Spanish version of "In the land of the blind, the one-eyed man is king":

En tierra de ciegos, el tuerto es rey.

This is splendid Spanish, concise yet lilting, but that's not what catches your eye. It is *el tuerto*, "the one-eyed man." Were there so many such men in long-ago Spain that they needed their very own noun? What about the French? The dictionary informs you that one-eyedness in France is indeed a substantive fact: *le borgne*. What's more, the condition seems to have been rampant among the French, for their version of the proverb is in the plural:

Au royaume des aveugles, les borgnes sont rois.

Convinced you've come across a peculiarity among Latins, you seek to verify it in the Italian dictionary. But no. The Italians, ever surprising, have no noun for "one-eyed." They describe the affliction adjectively, as we do. Their adjective, a beauty, is *monocolo*.

Monocolo sounds like a monocle. The English dictionary agrees. Monocle comes from "monocular," "suited to one eye," from the Greek *monos*, meaning "sole," and the Latin *oculus*, meaning "eye." A monocular telescope, for example. "Of course," you say to the dog, "that's why binoculars are called binoculars." And so it goes, hour after hour, when you might be walking down by the pond, your two eyes filled with the images of goslings.

What I'm talking about here is a pleasant obsession. At times it can also be confusing, for the literal translation of one idiom can mean something quite different in another language. An American uses "in the wind" to mean "already under way." A Frenchman uses "in the wind" to describe a person who is "with it." A "with it" Italian, someone who is up on everything, is said to "have his hands in the dough." Yet a Spaniard with his "hands in the dough" isn't "with it" at all. He's simply been "caught red-handed."

The "red-handed" idiom reminds me that I've not only been confused from time to time, I've been disappointed. I learned this idiom as a child and always thought it meant getting caught with jam on your hands. I now know that "red" means blood, but I prefer my version to the truth. Other disappointments include:

(1) "To go on a lark."

For me, this was the merriest of phrases, as graceful as a lark describing the air. I was not pleased to learn that "lark" comes from the Old Norse *leika* (to sport or frolic).

(2) "Not enough room to swing a cat."

Although most of us don't visualize our idioms, I never heard this one without imagining someone holding a cartoon cat by the tail and trying to swing it around the room. In this case, "cat" doesn't mean cat, it's short for the whip, cat-o'-nine-tails.

(3) "Don't cast your pearls before swine."

This biblical advice intrigued me, because of the variations in other languages. The French speak of pearls, but they also say, "It's foolish to squander roses on pigs." The Spanish warn against throwing *margaritas* at the pigs. A *margarita* is a daisy in Spain, and for a moment I took pleasure in the thought of pink pigs being flogged by flowers. But something nagged. Finally, an old children's poem came to mind:

> Although my name is Marguerite,
> And Marguerite means pearl,
> No one thinks that I am sweet —
> For I'm the middle girl.

Sure enough. Though the ordinary Spanish word for "pearl" is *perla*, the jewel is sometimes called a *margarita*. And that brings us right back to Matthew 7:6.

I speak of disappointments, but what are they to the myriad delights? Animal languages, for example.

An American cat goes purrr-r-r. A French cat goes *ronron*.

Ronronnement describes the purring. While an American cat says meow, a French cat says *miaou*. A French dog says *oua! oua!* A horse's whinny is *un hennissement*. A cow's moo is *un beuglement*.

An Italian cat says *miagolio*. An Italian dog says *bau! bau!* An Italian moo is, inexplicably, *un muggito*.

A Spanish cat sounds just like an American cat. It says *miau*. However, a Spanish bark is *¡guau guau!* A Spanish sheep doesn't say ba-a-a-a-a. It says *be-e-e-e-e*.

Another pleasure, every bit as useful as the study of animal languages, is the perusal of mottos.

Great families in Great Britain once amused themselves by choosing Latin mottos that were puns on the family names. For example, *Flores curat Deus* (God takes care of the flowers) is the motto of the Flowers family.

The Prince of Wales's motto is not only a pun, it's not Latin. It's *Ich dien*, German for "I serve."

In our country few families boast mottos, but all states do. Latin is the favored language:

> *Ad astra per aspera.* (Kansas)
> To the stars through difficulties.

> *Montani semper liberi.* (West Virginia)
> Mountaineers are always free.

> *Ense petit placidam sub libertate quietem.* (Massachusetts)
> By the sword we seek peace, but peace only under liberty.

Michigan's motto is also Latin, but not so solemn.

> *Si quaeris peninsulam amoenam, circumspice.*

If you seek a pleasant peninsula, look about you.

Montana's motto is Spanish.

> *Oro y plata.*
> Gold and silver.

Minnesota's motto is French.

> *L'Etoile du nord.*
> The star of the north.

One of Maryland's mottos is Italian.

> *Fatti maschii, parole femine.*
> Manly deeds, womanly words.

Hawaii's motto is Hawaiian.

> *Ua mau ke ea o ka aina i ka pono.*
> The life of the land is perpetuated in righteousness.

The best mottos of all belonged to private citizens:

> *Ancora imparo.* — Michelangelo
> I still learn.
>
> *Que sais-je?* — Montaigne
> What do I know?

Mottos are fine, but some other words and phrases I've unearthed should have been left in the dark.

> *Melancholy,* one of the loveliest words in the English language, comes from the Greek words meaning "black bile."
>
> *Camelot* means "peddler" in French.
>
> *Fourragère* is French for the ornamental braided cord looped under the left arm and attached to the shoulder of a uniform.
>
> *Guzunder* in England means "chamber pot," because it guzunder the bed.

It's quite all right to collect odd bits of information, but it's not all right to talk about them, for their effect on a conversation is dismal:

> "Speaking of *Mata Hari,* did you know that this is a Malay term meaning 'eye of the day' or 'sun'?"
>
> "*Gung ho,* by the way, is a Chinese phrase for 'work together.'"
>
> "You'd never guess what the lower section of the Norwegian legislature is called. The *Odelsting!*"

These conversational offerings are received with such dismay that I've learned to keep my discoveries to myself. Meantime, the secret scavenging goes on. The eye skims down a page and scoops up *haiku!*—a three-line poem of seventeen syllables. *Mahjong!* — "sparrow" in Chinese. *Mehr Licht!* ("More light!") — Goethe's last words. *Numdah!* — Anglo-Indian for the felt pad used under a saddle. *Selamat djalan!* — Malay for "Goodbye to you who are leaving!" *Selamat tinggal!* — Malay for "Goodbye to you who are staying!"

In the end, I've simply gathered thousands of pieces of a jigsaw puzzle that should make a picture but do not. In the process, though, I've developed a point of view about words and phrases and the people who use them. Before we get into that, I suppose it's high time to tackle definitions.

First, the idiom. It comes from a Greek word, *idios*, which means "proper" or "peculiar to one's self." In the broad sense it refers to a language or dialect, or to the way in which a language is put together. In the narrow sense (the way I use it), it means an accepted word or expression that *almost always has a meaning different from its literal meaning:* "I'm hopping mad." "You're crazy as a loon."

In a way, idioms become a code, a language within a language, designed to mystify outsiders and intensify the feelings of kinship among members of the tribe. Idioms defy classification, unless you'll settle for this: some make sense, some don't. Their original purpose was to give wit and intrigue to a language, but in use, idioms lose their impact. When you tell me that somebody's down and out, I don't visualize a boxer kayoed in a ring.

Next, the proverb. I look at it as a special kind of idiom, though it refuses to stay within the confines of a single language. In the Bible, a proverb is a story or saying containing a profound truth in disguise. It's similar to a parable or an allegory. In ordinary usage, a proverb is simply a short saying that expresses a generally accepted truth or fact, usually in an allegorical style.

Unlike idioms, proverbs are easy to put in their place. I

divide them all into two categories: Good Advice and Wise Observation. The advice or the observation can be sincere or cynical. Most of the time I find myself on the side of the cynics, all those anonymous cranks, for their aim is to rob us of our least appealing vices: pomposity and hypocrisy. This Spanish proverb sums it up nicely:

> *Dineros, no consejos.*
> (Give me) money, not advice.

It's been suggested that proverbs are a teaching device, and I suppose it's true, but the joy they give us is a sense of connection with other human beings. Proverbs affirm what we know of the human condition and make us feel less alone as we spin, God knows to what purpose, on our dazzling planet.

Of course, there are other ways to characterize expressions. An aphorism, an adage, and a saw are all synonymous with a proverb. An apothegm is close, but it's always a terse and pointed phrase. An epigram is terse, pointed, and witty. A maxim pulls itself a little apart from the others. It's usually a dignified statement of truth or a rule of conduct and doesn't involve itself in spilt milk and high horses.

When I first started this project, I assumed that the proverbs, idioms, and maxims of each language would dramatize the national characteristics. Well, they don't. There are minor differences, which I'll take up later in the book, but when it comes to matters of the heart and soul, God, gossip, babies, rainfall, and politicians, we the people of the world think alike. Not only that, we always have. "A liar should have a good memory," says a Roman sage to his dinner guests. Nearly two thousand years later we nod in agreement.

The study of common language should take place wherever voices babble. Instead, most writers of books about words get their information from other books. Black words on white paper have greater weight than words rocketing through the air. Besides, the books are fun to read.

Some are prudish. I have a handsome little French-English dictionary that denies the existence of prostitution. It also features a line drawing of a man to illustrate, in some detail, the parts of the body. Rather than point to parts they'd rather not name, the editors have dressed Monsieur in a bathing suit.

Some reference books are chivalrous. In one of my books of foreign phrases, the Italian word *cicisbeo* is defined as "the recognized gallant of a married lady." We've lost this use of the word "gallant" and I'm sorry. The same book also defines the Spanish word *hidalgo* as "a nobleman of the lower class," an odd definition, but quite accurate. Sometimes definitions don't define. The French word *miroton,* for example, means "beef collops smothered in onions." It sounds mighty good, but I had to look up "collop." It's "a piece of meat made tender by beating."

All people who write about words seek perfection and never find it. Samuel Johnson, the epitome of arrogance, becomes pensive and defensive in the preface to his dictionary:

> No dictionary of a living tongue ever can be perfect, since while it is hastening to publication, some words are budding and some falling away.

Other writers about words are also apologetic about the imperfections and errors in their writings. What amazes me is that the errors are so few, so unimportant. If a scholar in Barcelona, writing a treatise on English aphorisms, tells me that "lowe is blind," it makes me smile, but it doesn't diminish my affection for the writer or his field of endeavor. People rarely get rich and famous researching words. It's a labor of "lowe."

For centuries scholars studied all the world's languages, living and dead, in a valiant effort to prove that once upon a time, we all spoke the same tongue. The premise is a beautiful lie. Our only solace is knowing that even though we never shared the same language, we have often shared the same thoughts. It's my good fortune that these shared thoughts are so often expressed in different ways. For this is the basis of my book.

FAIR-WIND FRIENDS AND GILDED FISH AND OTHER SPANISH PLEASURES

Spaniards not only swear better than we do, they use idioms and proverbs more often and with greater glee. The number of phrases they can choose from is astonishing. The book *Refranero General Ideológico Español*, for example, lists 65,000 Spanish proverbs, collected by Luis Martínez Kleiser. In the Introduction, this distinguished scholar doesn't celebrate the treasures he has so carefully assembled. Instead he works himself up into a fine Spanish rage. Why? Spaniards, out of laziness and cussedness, aren't creating new proverbs fast enough. They are, he says, living on their linguistic savings, merrily spending their capital, while old proverbs continue to exist like pieces in a museum.

The man is right. There is a paucity of new proverbs in Spain, and no wonder. A language can accept just so many proverbs and idioms before it becomes preachy and arch. Since Spaniards refuse to give up the good old sayings, few new ones are being invented.

I'm not worried. The inherited capital of the language is so vast that its richness is assured for generations. We have only to savor its delights and quirks.

First the quirks. Toes, in Spanish, are "the fingers of the feet." Rattlesnakes are called "jingle bells." There is an adjective, *goloso*, to describe a lover of sweets, and a noun, *el alta*, that means either a discharge from a hospital or a certificate of induction into active service. The slang expression *pelar la pava* (to pluck the turkey) means "to make love at a window," a pastime I had not, until now, thought much about.

Odd expressions like these only serve to endear a language of awesome elegance and wit. Those who plan to master it, which isn't as easy as it's cracked up to be, will be relieved to know that many of the Spaniards' best idioms are ones they share with us.

A feeble-minded American is often called "touched." An equally afflicted Spaniard is called *un poco tocado*. (The *poco* softens the description, equivalent to an American saying, "poor soul.")

The sad and splendid phrase "What's done is done" is just as devastating in Spanish: *Lo hecho, hecho está*.

Americans and Spaniards both cry crocodile tears. Both lead a dog's life, take the bull by the horns, receive a lion's share, and leave with the tail between the legs. We both speak of a swan song and a stroke of luck, and we both know that all that glitters is not gold.

We share the notion of a seventh heaven. We both break the ice, clear the decks for action, swallow our pride, and have one foot in the grave. On occasion we both bite the dust.

On the other hand, an American has crow's feet, while a Spaniard has rooster feet. (*Pata de gallo*, or "rooster's foot," can also mean a blunder.) A Spaniard isn't a fair-weather friend. He's a fair-wind friend. And he doesn't take the wind out of your sails. He quenches your fires.

An American drowns his sorrow in drink. A Spaniard drowns his griefs in wine, or so the saying goes. Brandy is the choice of a Spaniard who's serious about it.

In Spain a fish isn't browned in a pan, it's gilded. And speaking of fish as the Spanish do, the verb is *pescar* (to fish). The catch is *la pesca*. The living fish is *el pez*. What ends up on your plate is *el pescado* (literally, "the fished"). If Spain were China, you could order your *pez* from the fish tank in the restaurant, and later eat *pescado,* after it had been killed and gilded.

The Church has contributed some fine phrases to Spanish. A "baker's dozen" is a "friar's dozen." "Selling like hot cakes" becomes "selling like holy bread." Thanks to Catholicism, the soul floats freely through the language. A Spaniard is the soul, not the life, of a party. And while an American gives up the ghost, a Spaniard surrenders his soul. There is, incidentally, a phrase for the instant of surrender: *El último trance* (the last moment of life).

"As the Devil carries off a soul" is the Spanish way of saying "like a bat out of hell." Their idiom is adequate, but it lacks the urgency, the sudden flutter of wings, of this grand American expression.

Other Spanish expressions, however, are more entrancing than their American counterparts. An American burns the midnight oil; a Spaniard burns his eyelashes. An American goes to pieces; a Spaniard loses his stirrups. When the room is stuffy, a Spaniard goes out for free air, emphasizing the difference between air trapped in a room and air that is free to meander around the planet. I like "free" better than our "fresh" or "open."

I like the gentle, falling sound of the Spanish term for snow-flake, *copo de nieve* (cup of snow). And I'd rather call a peacock *el pavo real* (the royal turkey).

Rhyming, the device used to make good advice easy to remember, is as tiresome in Spanish as it is in English. Once in a while the same proverb rhymes obediently in both languages. Thus "A friend in need is a friend indeed" becomes *Amigo en la adversidad es amigo de verdad.*

The Spanish have made a dreadful rhyme out of the idea expressed in "You can't get a leopard to change his spots": *Genio y figura hasta la sepultura* (Face and disposition stay with you till the grave). They also rhyme their version of "Rome wasn't built in a day." It is: *No se ganó Zamora en una hora* (Zamora wasn't won in an hour). If the battle had taken place in Seville, the saying would be, no doubt, *No se ganó Sevilla en un día*.

Sometimes the Spaniards go further than we do to dramatize the truth. We throw cold water on somebody's plans. They throw a *jar* of cold water, which sounds more fiendish. Our advice is not to look a gift horse in the mouth. Their advice is not to look at a gift horse's teeth, which is more to the point.

There's only one Spanish saying I've come across that doesn't make any sense. It's usually given as the equivalent of "That's locking the barn door after the horse is stolen." And it is: "That's feeding barley to the tail when the donkey is dead." Why the tail? Why not just "feeding barley to the donkey when it's already dead"? Perhaps the Spanish mean to describe a complete nincompoop — someone who would lock the house door after the horse had been stolen from the barn.

There's another Spanish saying that makes perfect sense, but I'm unable to paraphrase it in English. It is "to look for five legs on a four-legged cat." It's supposed to mean "to pick a quarrel," but that's not right. I've met exasperating people who weren't picking a quarrel. They were just looking for the fifth leg on the cat.

All the idioms and proverbs I've mentioned so far are from Spain's Spanish. I've left the linguistic peculiarities of Latin America untouched. For it is a frightening territory where idioms drift across borders and marry the locals; where words surge and merge and sometimes collide head on. Though it's been my intention to avoid the fray, I can't resist mentioning a few phrases I like.

For example, a Venezuelan isn't a fish out of water, he's a cockroach at a chicken dance. And while an American is caught red-handed, a Guatemalan is caught with the chicken under his arm.

"He kicked the bucket" is an engaging American expression. Irreverent but powerful. Especially so when it's compared to the Nicaraguan version: "He peeled the garlic." Or to the Salvadorian version — so sad: "He tied up his bundle."

Mexico contributes some jollier sayings. There, money does more than talk, it makes the monkey dance. And while we say, "Every dog has his day," they say, "Every little chapel has its little fiesta." A Mexican doesn't think he's hot stuff. He thinks he's the divine egret. And he's never left flat broke, he's left without John *or* the chickens.

In Spain, *¡Hay moros en la costa!* or "There are Moors on the coast!" is equivalent to "Jiggers!" or "Jiggers, the cops!" It's interesting to see what happened to those Moors when they reached Latin America. In El Salvador, "There are parakeets in the cornfield!" In Honduras, "There are parakeets on the mountain!" In Nicaragua, "There are parakeets on the hill!" And if a Nicaraguan senses extraordinary danger, he says, "There are parakeets on the hill *and* Moors on the coast!"

Now, back to Spain. On the following pages you'll find some of my favorite Spanish idioms and their American counterparts. But before you look ahead, contemplate these old Spanish sayings. We have nothing like them in English.

Aprovecha gaviota que no hay otra.
Appreciate the seagull as if there were no other.

Al amigo su vicio.
To each friend his vice.

A pobreza no hay verguenza.
There is no shame in poverty.

No hay quince años feos.
There are no ugly fifteen-year-olds.

A final thought: An American gives birth. A Spaniard gives light.

SPANISH IDIOMS ABOUT THE GREAT OUTDOORS

TO PUT SOMEONE IN THE CLOUDS.
Ponerlo por las nubes.

"To praise someone to the skies." Both idioms suggest enough adulation to turn a mortal into a god. A Spaniard also puts someone in the stars, and sometimes, over the stars.

TO THROW FLOWERS.
Echar flores.

Although this expression is very theatrical — red carnations flung at the beaming diva — it can't compete with our phrase for excessive praise: "to butter somebody up." The two idioms aren't quite equivalent. Throwing flowers can be innocent blarney, while the person who butters you up is usually after something.

IT'S RAINING JUGS!
¡Está lloviendo a cántaros!

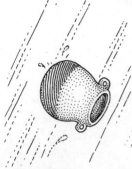

It may be raining jugs in Spain, but in France, it's raining ropes. In Italy, it's raining water basins. Sometimes it rains pitchforks in America, but usually it's cats and dogs.

THE HEALTH OF A ROCK.
Salud de piedra.

Spaniards also talk about *salud de hierro,* or "health of iron." Both phrases describe exuberant health, impressive endurance. In other words, an "iron constitution."

TO SCREAM AT THE SKY.
Poner el grito en el cielo.

We usually scream, too, at about the time we "hit the ceiling."

TO FALL ASLEEP ON YOUR LAURELS.
Dormirse en sus laureles.

We are content to rest on them.

LIFE ISN'T A ROSE PATH.
La vida no es senda de rosas.

It's no bed of roses either. Of course, nobody promised anybody a rose garden.

SPANISH IDIOMS ABOUT FOREIGN PEOPLE AND PLACES

TO PLAY THE INDIAN.
Hacer el indio.

"To play the fool." The idiom expresses a prejudice which disappeared when Spain lost its empire in the Americas. The prejudice against gypsies, however, still flourishes, in language as well as action. The word "gypsy," *gitano,* can be used as an adjective to mean "sly," "artful," or what my dictionary calls "honey-mouthed." The verb *gitanear* means "to wheedle or cajole." A *gitanada* is a "mean, contemptible trick." The Spanish gypsy's response to this is called *flamenco.* A scream of rage transformed into art.

THAT'S A CHINESE STORY!
¡Eso es un cuento chino!

"A tall tale."

TO PLAY THE SWEDE.
Hacer el sueco.

"To play dumb"; pretend not to understand. A Bolivian, incidentally, doesn't play the Swede, he plays the Italian. A Colombian plays the Englishman. A Mexican plays the duck.

SPEAK OF THE FALL OF ROME IT APPEARS AT THE DOOR.
Hablando del ruina de Roma por la puerta asoma.

> "Speak of the devil . . ."

IN THE AMERICAN STYLE.
A la americana.

> Occasionally, it means "to go Dutch."
> In parts of Latin America, the term is *ir a la inglesa* (to go English).

SPANISH IDIOMS ABOUT FOOD AND DRINK

IT'S NEITHER CORN LIQUOR NOR LEMONADE.
Ni chicha ni limonada.

> "It's neither fish nor fowl." It can also mean that nothing came of it, nothing happened. *Chicha*, the word for corn liquor, also means "flesh." If a Spaniard says that you have very few *chichas*, he means that you are nothing but skin and bones. *Una calma chicha* is a boating term. It means "a dead calm."

TO BURN IN YOUR OWN SAUCE.
Quemarse en su propia salsa.

> We don't burn. We just "stew in our own juice." An Italian seethes in his own way: he cooks in his own broth.

CLEARER THAN WATER.
Mas claro el agua.

> We say, "It's clear as crystal," which is
> very clear indeed, and "plain as day,"
> which is murky. It means, perhaps,
> "plain as daylight," or "as apparent as
> something seen in daylight," or "as easy
> to comprehend as an ordinary day."
> *¿Quién sabe?*

TO DROWN IN A GLASS OF WATER.
Ahogarse en un vaso de agua.

> To get all upset over nothing; to create
> "a tempest in a teapot."

THE APPLE OF DISCORD.
La manzana de la discordia.

> In Greek mythology, Paris awarded this
> golden apple, inscribed "to the fairest,"
> to Aphrodite — the first link in a chain
> of events that led to the Trojan War. To
> us, this apple of discord is merely "the
> bone of contention."

TO BE CAUGHT WITH YOUR HANDS IN THE DOUGH.
Cogerlo con las manos en la masa.

> "To be caught red-handed." The Spanish
> idiom would make more sense if
> "dough" meant "money," but it doesn't.

COFFEE STATESMEN.
Los estadistas de café.

> This refers to the gentlemen who sit
> over coffee in their cafés and clubs,

discussing affairs of state. "Armchair strategists," all.

GO FRY ASPARAGUS!
¡Véte a freír esparragos!

Or, "Go fly a kite!" The American kite was named after the bird of the same name, a type of falcon with a long forked tail. The Spaniards call a kite a "comet."

TO GIVE SOMEONE SQUASHES.
Darle calabazas.

"To give someone the gate." The squash in Spain is not held in great esteem. The word is used to mean "stupid." To "receive a squash" is to get a failing mark in an examination.

TO BE CAKES AND PAINTED BREAD.
Ser tortas y pan pintado.

"Painted bread" is a sweet bread with swirls of icing. The idiom refers to something that's "child's play," "easy as pie." (I don't think pies are easy, but my grandmother did. She, and the other Idaho farm wives, made two or three pies every morning. They were served to the family and farmhands as breakfast dessert.)

WHERE SIX CAN EAT, SEVEN CAN EAT.
Donde comen seis, comen siete.

> "There's always room for one more."

TO (BOTH) CHEW ON ONE CANDY.
Morder en un confite.

> "To be thick as thieves."

IT'S THE FINAL DROP THAT MAKES THE GLASS
OVERFLOW.
La última gota es la que hace rebosar el vaso.

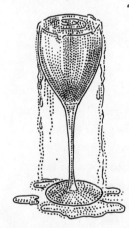

"It's the final straw that breaks the camel's back." Or simply, "That's the final straw!" This American proverb is one of several that get their tails chopped off in ordinary usage:

> "It's an ill wind . . ."
> "Spare the rod . . ."
> "Too many cooks . . ."

WITH THEE, A LOAF OF BREAD, AND AN ONION.
Contigo, pan y cebolla.

> This is the homely Spanish version of ". . . A Jug of Wine, a Loaf of Bread — and Thou / Beside me singing in the Wilderness . . ."

SPANISH IDIOMS ABOUT HOUSES AND FARMS

TO THROW STONES AT YOUR OWN ROOF.
Tirar piedras contra su propio tejado.

> The Spanish idiom is glum. Ours is funny: "To cut off your nose to spite your face."

TO GO OUT FOR WOOL AND COME HOME SHORN.
Ir por lana y volver esquilado.

> "To have the tables turned on you."

TO LEAVE SOMEONE PLANTED.
Dejarlo plantado.

> "To leave someone flat." I don't know which idiom is the finer. "Flat" is how we feel when we've been left: sprawled out, knocked for a loop. But "planted" also says a lot: up to here in dirt, immobilized, feeling the perfect fool.

TO BE LEFT IN A FINE EGGPLANT PATCH.
Quedarse en un buen berenjenal.

> How exasperating. It's like "being left in a jam." The French equivalent, *se fourrer dans un guêpier* (to be shoved into a wasps' nest), goes beyond exasperation into the realm of panic.

THREE TO A SACK AND THE SACK IS ON THE GROUND.
Tres al saco y el saco en tierra.

> Or, "Too many cooks spoil the broth."

Two to a sack is the proper number:
one to hold the sack open, one to throw
the apples in.

TO THROW THE HOUSE OUT THE WINDOW.
Echar la casa por la ventana.

It sounds like fun, and so it should. It
means "to shoot the works."

HE DOESN'T FALL ASLEEP IN THE STRAW.
No se duerme en las pajas.

"He doesn't let the grass grow under his
feet." Even though straw is good to
sleep on, the word usually means
"worthless." In Spanish, "to quarrel
over straws" is to quarrel over trifles.
We say, "I don't give a straw," and
"he's just a straw man." In both France
and Italy, a "straw man" means a
clown. In France, it's *le paillasse.* In
Italy, *il pagliaccio.*

A STRAW WIDOW.
La viuda de paja.

The American equivalent is "a grass
widow," a divorced woman. No one
knows where the grass or straw
references came from. It's been
suggested that people once thought that
no man would ever divorce his wife

unless she'd been caught frolicking in the grass, or the hayloft.

TO MAKE YOUR AUGUST.
Hacer su agosto.

This refers to an August harvest, and it means "to make a killing," "to rake it in."

THE JOY IS IN THE WELL.
El gozo en el pozo.

It means that your joy, your hopes, your plans have all gone "down the drain." *Alegría* is a more elegant word for joy or gaiety, but *gozo* has its charms, sensuous and sensual. *Pozo* means a ditch, as well as a well, and it's used in this sense in the saying *El muerto al pozo y el vivo al gozo,* "The corpse to the ditch and the living to their pleasure." A robust interpretation of the advice in Matthew: "Let the dead bury the dead."

TO MISTAKE THE RADISH FOR THE LEAVES.
Tomar el rábano por las hojas.

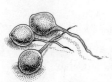

"To jump to the wrong conclusion." I like the American idiom. The earnest listener, nodding his head, then slowly bending his knees and pushing off for a valiant leap, landing with a thud on the wrong idea.

SPANISH IDIOMS ABOUT THE BODY, INCLUDING THE WINGS, PAWS, AND TAIL

I WOULDN'T WANT TO BE IN YOUR SKIN.
No quisiera estar en su pellejo.

> We feel the same way, but express ourselves less dramatically: "I wouldn't want to be in your shoes."

TO TAKE IT TO CHEST.
Tomar a pecho.

> "To take it to heart." *Pecho* is an important word in Spanish. It means chest, breast, courage, fortitude. As a musical term, it refers to the quality of a voice. Instead of opening his heart to you, a Spaniard opens his chest. It's a shame this fine strong word doesn't lend itself to love songs. The Spaniard's three-syllable heart, *cor-a-zón,* is chanted so often that a new word would be oh so welcome.

TO STRETCH OUT YOUR PAW.
Estirar la pata.

> "To turn in your chips," "kick the bucket," "give up the ghost." *Estirar* not only means to stretch, but also "to put on airs," referring, I suppose, to

someone who stretches his spine to
achieve a tall and haughty stance.

TO BE ALL PAWS UP.
Estar todo patas arriba.
> "To be topsy-turvy."

HEARTS, ARISE!
¡Arriba, los corazones!
> "Chin up!" or "Chins up!" as the case
> may be. Speaking of the chin, the
> Spaniards usually call it *la barba*, which
> also means "the beard."

TO HAVE YOUR HEART IN YOUR HAND.
Tener el corazón en la mano.
> "To wear your heart on your sleeve."
> Also, when a Spaniard is suddenly
> startled or frightened, his heart isn't in
> his mouth, it's in his fist.

TO BURN YOUR EYELASHES.
Quemarse las pestañas.
> "To burn the midnight oil." A person's
> eyelashes get singed when he or she
> dozes off too close to the candle. "To
> burn your eyebrows" is another version
> of the idiom.

IT STICKS TO YOUR KIDNEY.
Se pega al riñon.

The phrase refers to hearty food, the
kind that "sticks to your ribs." In

Spanish, "to have kidneys" means to have courage. If you have a "well-covered kidney," it means you are well-off. We used to use the word to mean "character." A person was described as "someone of good kidney." The term is now out of fashion and I'm glad.

TO TOSS A GRAY HAIR IN THE AIR.
Echar una cana al aire.

"To go on a spree," "on a lark," "out on the town." Since the hair that gets tossed is gray, you might assume the expression refers to old folks, but it doesn't. A spree in Spain usually involves a lot of people. When a couple goes out, they've got the children with them, and his parents, her aunt, and three cousins who are visiting from Seville.

TO SLAM THE DOOR ON YOUR NOSTRILS.
Cerrarle la puerta en las narices.

We're not quite so rude. We "slam the door in your face."

TO GRAB SOMEONE'S HAIR.
Tomarle el pelo a uno.

In Spain, children sometimes do it literally, adults do it figuratively. It means "to pull someone's leg." We use a similar phrase, a "hair-pulling contest," to describe a fracas between two

women. The phrase isn't used much,
but the contests can still be seen late at
night in old movies when enraged
French cancan dancers or feisty whores
in Old West saloons pummel each
other.

TO GO FROM MOUTH TO MOUTH.
Andar de boca en boca.

It refers to something that's common
knowledge. Sometimes it refers to a
person who is "the talk of the town."

TO FALL MOUTH DOWN.
Caerse boca abajo.

We fall "face down." The Spaniard
seems preoccupied with his mouth when
he takes a spill. Instead of saying, "I fell
on my face!" he says, "I fell on my
lips!"

TO HAVE FALLEN EARS.
Estar con las orejas caídas.

The image is a dejected hound. It means
"to be crestfallen."

GIVE HIM A HAND AND HE TAKES A FOOT.
Le da la mano y se toma el pie.

We know him well. "If you give him an
inch, he'll take a mile."

TO KNOW SOMETHING LIKE THE PALM OF YOUR HAND.
Conocer una cosa como la palma de la mano.

> To know something "from A to Z," or "like the back of your hand." It seems strange that we memorize the back of the hand, when the palm is more worthy of contemplation.

TO BE STUCK WITH THE CORPSE.
Cargar con el muerto.

> It means "to be left holding the bag." The Spanish idiom reminds me of what happened to some friends of friends of mine in Spain many years ago. They were an American couple in their sixties who spent every summer camping in the mountains of Andalusia. They drove a little truck and the man's old but sprightly mother always came along on the trip. One morning, in the middle of nowhere, the couple awoke to discover that the aged parent had died in her sleep. The grief-stricken couple drove to the nearest village, where sympathetic villagers hammered together a coffin out of old packing crates. When *la muerta* was safely on board, the couple started the long drive to Madrid to catch a plane back to the States. Four hours later they stopped for lunch, and while they were in the cafe, *somebody stole the truck.*

HE FLIES WITH HIS OWN WINGS.
Vuela con sus propias alas.

> "He stands on his own two feet" means the same thing, but with a difference. The American is standing there, earthbound. The Spaniard is soaring.

SHE HAS HIM IN HER FIST.
Lo tiene en un puño.

> The way we see it, she has him "under her thumb."

FLESH AND BONE.
Carne y hueso.

> Your relatives. Your "flesh and blood."

TO BE ALIVE AND WAGGING YOUR TAIL.
Estar vivo y coleando.

> "To be alive and kicking." Our idiom is fine and frisky, but their idiom warms the heart, for it symbolizes the most engaging of all Spanish qualities, the ability to savor the moment.

SPANISH IDIOMS ABOUT ANIMALS, BIRDS, FISH, AND BUGS

I HAVE A ROOSTER IN MY THROAT.
Tengo un gallo en la garganta.

To an American, it's a frog. To a
Frenchman, it's a cat. Whatever it is, it
seems to be alive.

A MONKEY DRESSED IN SILK IS STILL A MONKEY.
Aunque la mona se vista de seda, mona se queda.

"Clothes don't make the man." Or, "You
can't make a silk purse out of a sow's
ear."

HEN FLESH.
Carne de gallina.

"Goose bumps." The Spanish also speak
of "the hen that laid the golden eggs."
Gallina ciega (blind hen) is the game we
call blindman's buff.

THERE ARE MANY WAYS TO KILL FLEAS.
Hay muchos modos de matar pulgas.

> "There's more than one way to skin a cat." Let's ignore the American phrase and talk about Spanish fleas. When a person "has fleas," it means he's jumpy, restless. "To have bad fleas" means to be touchy and ill-tempered.

TO PUT THE BELL ON THE CAT.
Poner el cascabel al gato.

> The English use the phrase "belling the cat," and occasionally it's heard in America, but most of the time we court greater danger by trying to "beard the lion." The Spanish word for cat also means a native of Madrid, a pickpocket, a petty thief, or someone tricky and shrewd. *Vender gato por liebre* (to sell cat for hare) means to hoodwink someone. *Gato* has been turned into a verb, *gatear*. It means to creep and it's said of babies.

TO BE LEFT ON THE HORNS OF THE BULL.
Dejar en las astas del toro.

> "To be left up in the air," or "in a lurch." "Lurch" is a cribbage term. It's a position you don't want to get into.

TO TOSS OUT TOADS AND SNAKES.
Echar sapos y culebras.

> The Spaniards are very good at it. We

aren't, but at least our idiom has color:
"to swear a blue streak."

TO BE A FAT FISH.
Ser un pez gordo.

We describe this sort of person as big.
Either a wheel or a shot or a gun.

A BIRD IN THE HAND IS WORTH MORE THAN A HUNDRED FLYING.
Más vale pájaro en mano que cien volando.

The imagery here is so beautiful, it
makes our "two in the bush" version of
the proverb seem downright blunt.
Since the Spanish idiom is perfect,
there's no excuse for the mysterious
alternate expression sometimes heard in
Spain: "A bird in the hand is worth
more than a vulture flying."

GO SEE ANOTHER DOG WITH THAT BONE!
¡Véte a otro perro con ese hueso!

"Go jump in the lake!" "Tell it to the
marines!" "Go fly a kite!" How
innocent all these phrases sound.
Nowadays, our language of anger is

almost always vulgar. It's the same in
Spain.

**THE NEIGHBOR'S HEN LAYS MORE EGGS THAN MINE
DOES.**
La gallina del vecino pone más huevos que la mía.

> Not only that, "the grass is always
> greener on the other side of the fence."

HE'S A LIBRARY MOUSE.
Es un ratón de biblioteca.

> We call him a "bookworm."

TO PAY FOR THE DUCK.
Pagar el pato.

> It means "to be the fall guy," but there's
> more petulance in the Spanish
> expression. It's as if you and your
> friends went out on the town, ate the
> duck, drank the wine, broke the plates,
> and then they all walked off and left
> you with the bill.

IT WAS RICE AND DEAD ROOSTER.
Había arroz y gallo muerto.

> In other words, "a real spread." Wine,
> olives, salad, cheese, ham, shrimp,
> squid, crab, rice, chicken, fruit,
> pastries, and champagne. "Quite a
> clambake."

FLEEING FROM THE BULL, HE FELL INTO THE BROOK.
Huyendo del toro, cayó en el arroyo.

> "He jumped from the frying pan into the

fire." There's a funny Central American version of this: *salir de Guatemala y entrar en Guatepeor.* (to leave Guate-bad and go to Guate-worse).

SPANISH IDIOMS ABOUT MAYHEM, DEATH, AND DESTITUTION

TO DIE AT THE FOOT OF THE CANYON.
Morir al pie del cañón.

"To die with your boots on." Most of the time, the Spaniards die in the same ways we do. They die laughing. Someone looking forward to lunch is dying of hunger.

TO SINK YOURSELF.
Irse a pique.

"To go off the deep end."

TO LIVE BY THE CAP.
Vivir de gorra.

This seems to describe a street beggar's life, but it means "to be a deadbeat" or "a sponge." *Gorrear* (to cap) is to live as a parasite, and the fellow himself is called a *gorrero*. The French use the same imagery: *bonnetier* or *casquettier*. The beautiful hat called a *béret* in

France, and a *boina* in Spain, escapes
the stigma of these idioms, being too
soft and floppy to serve, even
figuratively, as a receptacle for coins.

TO LEAVE SOMEONE IN THE STREET.
Dejar a uno en la calle.

"To bleed somebody white," or "to take
somebody to the cleaners."

TO LOSE YOUR STIRRUPS.
Perder los estribos.

"To go to pieces." Our idiom is good, but
theirs is better. We may be lying in bits
on the floor, but the poor Spaniard is
galloping across the plains, the horse
deciding the direction. *Estribo* comes
from the verb *estribar* (to depend on).

TO BURN YOUR SHIPS.
Quemar sus naves.

We're more concerned about burning
our bridges behind us. A Frenchman
cuts his bridges. An Italian cuts his
bridges as he crosses. Everything has
been cut and burned. Now what?

TO BE BETWEEN THE SWORD AND THE WALL.
Estar entre la espada y la pared.

It's Errol Flynn pinned (only for a
moment) against the castle wall by
Basil Rathbone's quivering foil. Our
expression, "to have your back against

the wall," creates a different mood, one
of sadness and desperation.

Spanish Idioms About Saints and the Church

TO UNDRESS ONE SAINT IN ORDER TO DRESS ANOTHER.
Desnudar a uno santo para vestir a otro.

> Our saying is similar, but we're more
> specific about our saints: we "rob Peter
> to pay Paul."

TO BE LEFT TO DRESS SAINTS.
Quedarse para vestir santos.

> This refers to an unmarried woman, one
> who's been "left on the shelf." Dressing
> saints means to decorate the altars of
> the church. If a Spaniard spends too
> much time at it, there's a chance he or
> she will be labeled a *tragasantos* (a saint
> swallower), a sneering term for
> someone who is too devout.

TO KNOW SOMETHING LIKE THE HAIL MARY.
Saberlo como el avemaría.

> "To know something backwards and
> forwards." *En un avemaría* means "in a
> jiffy."

TO BE DANCING IN BETHLEHEM.
Estar bailando en Belén.

"To be daydreaming," or "woolgathering." *Belén,* the beautiful Spanish word for Bethlehem, is also the term used for a nativity scene. (We borrow the French word for cradle, a *crèche.*) *Belén* is an appropriate word, for the Spaniards often create a well-populated city around the Holy Family. I saw a breathtaking *belén* once that included Wise Men, angels, pigs, fighting bulls, knights in armor, and Velásquez infantas.

The Spaniards daydream in other ways. They can be in the clouds. On the moon. Or in a fig tree. Sometimes, they are in *Babia,* a mythical kingdom, Spain's never-never land.

TO GIVE UP THE SOUL.
Entregar el alma.

We "give up the ghost." Our word "ghost" has taken on a frail, wispy quality because it's so often used to mean an apparition. It's from the Anglo-Saxon *gast* (spirit) and is related to the Icelandic *geisa,* which means "to rage as fire," a fascinating way to describe the machination of the human spirit.

SAINT MARTIN'S LITTLE SUMMER.
El veranillo de San Martín.

"Indian summer." Saint Martin's feast

day is November 11, and a spell of warm weather around that time is honored by his name. This term is indicative of the Spaniard's attitude toward the saints, which is familial. The church itself is called *Nave de San Pedro*, Saint Peter's Ship. The phrase "He's not a saint I'm devoted to" means "He's not someone I especially like."

SPANISH IDIOMS ABOUT A GREEN OLD MAN, A CASTLE OF CARDS, ET CETERA

TO SEND OFF SPARKS.
Echar chispas.

We also use this phrase, but not as often as the Spaniards do. It means "to be good and mad," "hopping mad," "mad as a hornet." The word *chispa* also means "wit," "verve," "sparkle." *Estar chispa* means "to be tipsy." Just plain *¡chispas!* means "nuts!"

TO WATER THE FESTIVAL.
Aguar la fiesta.

"To rain on someone's parade," "to be a wet blanket."

IT'S LIKE TAKING IRON TO VISCAYA.
Es como llevar hierro a Viscaya.
>   Or "coals to Newcastle." In ancient
>   Greece, it was like sending owls to
>   Athens.

HE'S VERY MAN.
Es muy hombre.
>   We say he's "all man," or a "he-man."
>   Our expressions sound old-fashioned,
>   but the Spanish phrase is current and
>   complimentary. *¡Ea, hombre!* is a term of
>   casual affection and it's used, man, like
>   I don't know, man, a fill word.

PIANO WITH A LITTLE TAIL.
Piano de cola pequeño.
>   We call it a "baby grand," which is also
>   a droll expression.

A GREEN OLD MAN.
Un viejo verde.
>   "A dirty old man."

TO STRIKE WHILE THE IRON IS RED.
Batir el hierro cuando está al rojo.
>   We "strike while the iron is hot," thus
>   missing the splendid tension of the
>   smithy's shop, as the iron slowly turns
>   from black to ash gray to a glowing red.

DRESSED IN TWENTY-FIVE PINS.
Vestido de veinticinco alfileres.
>   We're "dressed to kill," so we can "go
>   out there and knock 'em dead."

TO HAVE A SCREW MISSING.

Faltarle un tornillo.

> An American screw is loose but not lost.
> Sometimes we lose our marbles.
> Sometimes we suffer a lack that isn't
> defined: we're "not all there."

A CASTLE OF CARDS.

Un castillo de naipes.

> "A house of cards." The Spaniards,
> incidentally, build castles in the air, but
> not in Spain. Chaucer said it for the rest
> of us: "Thou shall make castles then in
> Spain, / And dream of joy, all but in
> vain."

TO CONSULT YOUR PILLOW.
Consultar con la almohada.

> "To think it over," "to sleep on it." The Spanish idiom is rather cute. The discovery of anything cute in the language or the land always comes as a jolt.

HE DOESN'T NEED A GRANDMOTHER.
No necesita abuela.

> He doesn't need a grandmother to sing his praises, because "he toots his own horn."

TO COME THROUGH THE HOOP.
Pasar por el aro.

> "To fall into line." Our idiom is military. Theirs seems to describe the lion's act at the circus.

BLACK BEASTS AND LION'S TEETH AND OTHER FRENCH TRADITIONS

According to legend, when good Americans die they go to Paris. If so, one of their heavenly rewards is listening to the natives speak. For if the Germans have too many consonants, and the Spaniards too many vowels, the French have just the right balance. This exquisitely balanced language is then delivered with the grand Gallic twang that gives each *citoyen*, from the age of two, a voice of extraordinary resonance.

"Bring the garbage can back to the house, John Louis!" hollers the Parisian housewife, and to the foreigner passing by, the words are enchanting. The French are the people who christened the garbage can *la poubelle*. They call their skunk *une mouffette*. Their snorer is *un ronfleur*. French words sound pretty even when their meaning isn't.

> *Alouette! Gentille alouette!*
> *Alouette! Je te plumerai!*

> Skylark! Sweet skylark!
> Skylark! I'm going to pluck you!

The French not only speak the most beautiful of languages, they invent grand idioms. Sometimes they use colorful sayings for ideas we express matter-of-factly. The French idiom for "Let's get back to the subject" is *Revenons à nos moutons* (Let's get back to our sheep). The phrase comes up at business meetings in airless, fluorescent-lit conference rooms. For a moment, it evokes the pastoral image of strolling shepherds, deep in conversation, who have strayed too far from their flock.

The French have another colorful phrase that means "Get back to the subject!" or "Get your act together!" It is *Accordez vos violons!* (Tune your violins!)

At one time, the merchandise in used-clothing shops in France was hung on hooks high above the customers' heads. To inspect a garment, each shopper had to point and plead, *Décrochez-moi ça!* (Take that down for me!) That's why a French secondhand store used to be called "at the take-that-down-for-me."

The language is funny, sublime, and so universally admired that it comes as a shock to find small flaws. They exist. From France comes one of the uglier idioms: *Va te faire cuire un oeuf!* It sounds awful, and it means "Go cook yourself an egg!" To this, my reply is, "Oh, go fly a kite!" The famous precision of the language sometimes robs it of a colorful saying. "I laughed till I cried!" is splendid English. *Je riais aux larmes* (I laughed to tears) is more precise and less fine.

Sometimes the French *don't* have a word for it. For instance, it is impossible to translate the following sentence into French:

> "Young man, stop whistling at me!" hissed the pretty girl.

To whistle and to hiss are one and the same to the French. The hard-working verb is *siffler*.

Our lively idiom "This is a fine kettle of fish!" becomes bland in French: *En voilà une affaire!* (What a business!) Worse than bland is a French version of "A bird in the hand is worth two in the bush." It is: "Something you possess is worth more than two things you will have." *Alors!*

Diligent research could turn up other weaknesses in the language, but it gives greater pleasure to point out its merits. The French, for example, rhyme their proverbs more gracefully than the rest of us. My favorites are short and sweet.

> *A bon chat, bon rat.*
> To the good cat, a good rat.
>
> *Mieux vaut sagesse que richesse.*
> Wisdom is worth more than wealth.
>
> *Vouloir, c'est pouvoir.*
> To wish is to be able.

The French rhyme their version of "Speak of the Devil!": *Quand on parle du loup, on en voit la queue* (Speak of the wolf and you see his tail). In France, for the sake of the rhyme, a stitch in time saves more than nine. It saves a hundred: *Un point fait à temps en épargne cent.*

Even if you had no prior knowledge of the Frenchman's preoccupation with food and drink, the idioms of the language would soon make the point. We split the difference; the French divide a pear in two. To us, it's no bed of roses; to the French, it's not all honey. An American goes broke; a Frenchman drinks broth. The French version of "The game is up!" is "That's the last of the green beans!"

The green-bean idiom reminds me of a fine French custom, the annual celebration of each crop as it comes to market, when *toute la France* gives in to the pleasures of buying and eating and discussing the strawberries! The asparagus! The beans!

Although there is no great celebration of the cabbage harvest, the French are obsessed with *chou*. *Mon petit chou* is an everyday endearment. When a Frenchman is put out to pasture, he goes out to plant his cabbages. Instead of saying, "easy as pie," he says, "easy as cabbage." The French have even created a verb out of this vegetable: *chouchouter* (to pet or fondle). *Le chouchou de maman* is a mama's boy. *La chouchoute de papa* is a daddy's girl. *Le chouchou du prof* is a teacher's pet.

Clearly, the French have a *chou* fetish, though the vegetable seldom turns up at the restaurants I frequent. I've eaten cabbage only once in France, at the Brasserie Lipp in Paris, where it was made into sauerkraut and served with sausages. The meal was good, but far less memorable than the sign on the restaurant wall that said: PLEASE DON'T FEED SAUER-KRAUT TO YOUR DOG.

I've thought a lot about that sign. It didn't say PLEASE DON'T FEED YOUR DOG FROM THE TABLE. *All* French dogs get fed from the table, sometimes while sitting smugly on the banquette. Could it be that sauerkraut is upsetting to dogs? Was Lipp trying to head off trouble? If so, I wouldn't be surprised, for the French are devoted to canines. In America a dog is a pet. In England a dog is a prized possession. In France a dog is a member of the family, an amusing niece or errant nephew who is, by chance, furred and speechless.

It's not surprising then that the dog romps through the French language. *Entre chien et loup* (between dog and wolf) is the curious term for twilight. (If you must know, it's an old Latin phrase. It means the time of day when it is impossible, from afar, to distinguish between a dog and a wolf.) *Avoir du chien* (to have some quality of the dog) means to have style. We might call it "puttin' on the dog."

The French use many other animals idiomatically, but seldom in the same way that we do. When a French person is momentarily hoarse, he says, "I have a cat in my throat." Instead of saying, "Let sleeping dogs lie!" he says, "Don't arouse the sleeping cat!" There's a weed in France called "lion's tooth," *dent-de-lion,* which we've corrupted into "dandelion." When a Frenchman feels as if he's been made the patsy or the goat, he says, "You've made me the turkey of the farce!"

There is, finally, the Frenchman's pet peeve, or *bête noire,* a mysterious black beast that France has exported to the far corners of the world.

Using *bête noire* and other French phrases is supposed to give a touch of class to plain American speech. I don't much like this practice. It's *nouveau riche.* Carry the affectation to the extreme and it sounds silly.

> Dear Marjorie,
>
> *Entre nous,* Harry's threatened departure is a *fait accompli.* He left town last week with his latest *liaison,* a *passé* blonde with a whole *entourage* of *parvenu* relatives. Harry, with his usual *naïveté,* took them *en masse* to Antibes. He expects to meet the *crème de la crème* there, and of course the place is now hopelessly *bourgeois.* I hear they stopped in London *en route,* a real *faux pas* on Harry's part, since he ran into Serena Phipps-Smythe (last year's *petite amie*), and there was a scene at the Dorchester.
>
> I'm facing all this with my usual *savoir-faire.* Fortunately, here in Palm Beach we have great *esprit de corps.* So don't worry. I'll soon have my *joie de vivre* back. And — eventually — Harry.
>
> Meantime . . . love,
> Nora

Flinging French words on the English language is one thing. Adopting a foreign word to fill a need is quite another. We adopted *chi-chi* from the Anglo-Indian because there was no adjective in English to describe the characteristic. *Chi-chi* enriches our language. *Entre nous* doesn't.

When you're listening to a high-toned Frenchman give a solo performance of his language, with the nasal sounds humming along and the phrases all ending in dying falls, it is hard to believe that French had humble beginnings. When the armies of Julius Caesar conquered the Gauls around 50 B.C., the local language was doomed. Although a form of Gaelic is still spoken in Brittany, only about four hundred Gaulish words are still alive in modern France. The Gauls gradually learned Latin, but their new language didn't include all the poetic grandeur of the Roman intellectuals. It was the robust speech of the army of occupation. Many of the refined Greek and Latin words in contemporary French didn't arrive until the Renaissance — a handful of delicate herbs and spices for a hearty soldier's stew.

Given its boisterous beginnings, the language isn't as playful as you might imagine. *Houp-là!* is nice, but can it truly compare to "whoops-a-daisy"? Our "thingamabob" or "thingamajig" or "whatchamacallit" becomes simply *un truc*.

Though we invent livelier "play words," the French are better at pulling petals off a daisy. Their version of "He loves me . . . he loves me not" is filled with high drama. *Il m'aime un peu . . . beaucoup . . . passionnément . . . à la folie . . . pas du tout!* ("He loves me a little . . . a lot . . . passionately . . . madly . . . not at all!")

The French people like angels. They share our concepts of the fallen angel and the guardian angel and use the word as a term of affection, but that's only the beginning. When there's an awkward little pause in the conversation, the appropriate phrase is *Un ange passe,* "An angel is passing by." *Parler aux anges* has a pious ring, but it means "to talk to yourself." *Etre aux anges* (to be with the angels) is "to be walking on air." *Rire aux anges* (to smile at the angels) is either "to have a big silly grin on your face" or "to smile in your sleep."

French angels are not all sweetness and light. An abortionist is called an "angel maker." The phrase "someone's bad angel" refers to that person's talent for evil. There is also a heavenly way to refer to the sexual climax: *voir les anges* (to see angels).

Americans who speak French usually speak it wretchedly. However, a French friend once told me that while a Spanish or German accent grates on the French ear, an American or English accent sounds "rather sweet." Chaucer put it this way:

> Ful weel she soong the service dyvyne,
> Entuned in hir nose ful semely;
> And Frenssh she spak ful faire and fetisly,
> After the scole of Stratford atte Bowe
> For Frenssh of Parys was to hir unknowe.

Most of us sound as if we'd studied the language at that school in Stratford, not in Parys.

Outsiders have almost loved *La France* better than *Les Français.* This doesn't bother the French, but it bothers me. I can imagine the world without them, but I don't like it. In an attempt to beguile American francophobes, I offer these idioms:

> A Frenchman is never in the swim. He's in the bath.

He doesn't put his foot in his mouth. He puts his feet in his plate.

He doesn't get a chill. He gets a hot-and-cold.

He doesn't let his hair down. He unbuttons himself.

Other French idioms and their American equivalents are presented on the following pages. In grace and wit the two languages are well matched. Once in a while, though, you have to hand it to them:

> *Si jeunesse savait, si vieillesse pouvait.*
> If the young only knew. If the old only could.

FRENCH IDIOMS ABOUT FARMS, FARM ANIMALS, AND THE COUNTRYSIDE

DONKEY SKIN.
Peau d'âne.

A "sheepskin." A diploma.

THE MANGY SHEEP OF THE FAMILY.
La brebis galeuse de la famille.

This is supposed to be the same as "the black sheep of the family," but I

wonder. A black sheep is a rebel with a
twinkle in his eye. A mangy lady sheep
is merely forlorn.

DRENCHED LIKE A DUCK.
Trempé comme un canard.

Thoroughly drenched, like a "drowned
rat." The French clearly have never
looked at a duck in a rainstorm, with
the water running merrily off its back.
Faire un canard (to do a duck) means to
hit a wrong note. We've adopted the
word *canard* and use it with a sneer to
signify a nasty rumor, if not a bold-
faced lie. I'm glad we don't translate the
word. It saves us from "Your inference
that my client attempted to bribe the
Plumbers' Union is a duck! A mere
duck!"

THE FIELD IS FREE!
Le champ est libre!

And "the coast is clear," too.

TO SAVE THE GOAT AND THE CABBAGE.
Ménager la chèvre et le chou.

"To have your cake and eat it, too." The
French expression, which informs us
that goats are a menace to a cabbage
patch, is just one of many variations on
the *chou* theme. The French even graft
the name *chou* onto other vegetables.
Cauliflower is *chou-fleur*. Brussel sprouts

are *chou de Bruxelles*. Kale is *chou frisé*. They do allow spinach to have its own name, and they use it in a homey phrase to describe a small but welcome financial gain: *Ça mettra du beurre dans les épinards!* (That'll put some butter on the spinach!)

A PIG TRICK.
Un tour de cochon.

"A dirty trick" or "a bad turn." Just plain "pig" is an insult in either language. *Cochonnerie* means "filthiness" or "muck." "Guinea pig" sounds lovely in French: *cochon d'Inde*. This "pig of India" is no doubt sleek and white, and on feast days wears a silver harness and marigolds in its hair.

THE TURKEY IN THE FARCE.
Le dindon de la farce.

It sounds like the ding-dong of the farce, and that's close, for it means the fool, or the "patsy."

TO PUT HAY IN YOUR BOOTS.
Mettre du foin dans les bottes.

"To feather your nest." "To feather" is a dainty verb used so infrequently that it is in danger of floating away. Besides nests, what can you feather? Only oars.

TO CUT THE GRASS UNDER YOUR FEET.
Couper l'herbe sous les pieds.

> "To pull the rug out from under you."
> The French idiom gets the point across,
> but it lacks wit. Our idiom is full of
> surprise, flying feet, flailing arms.

A CHICKEN NEST.
Un nid de poule.

> The roads are full of them. It means "a
> pothole."

TO PROMISE MOUNTAINS AND MARVELS.
Promettre monts et merveilles.

> All we can do is "promise the moon," or
> sometimes "the moon and the stars."
> The Spaniard is far more down to earth.
> He promises you "gold and the Moors!"

TO PLAY JUMP-SHEEP.
Jouer à saute-mouton.

> When you played it, you called it "leap-
> frog."

ON THE STRAW.
Sur la paille.

> Reduced to sleeping on straw. In other
> words, "down and out." "On the skids"
> is another way of putting it. There's a
> lot of movement in that phrase and it's
> all downhill.

A STRAW FIRE.
Un feu de paille.

A fire that has no substance and burns out quickly. It's nothing more than a "flash in the pan." Our idiom describes the flash in the pan of a flintlock musket when it misfires, not — as I always thought — the fool's gold that flashed in the pans of gold miners. Back to straw. *Perdre son chapeau de paille* (to lose your straw hat) means to lose your virginity. It was said originally of French country boys who came to the big city to see the sights, make their fortunes, lose their hats.

TO TAKE THE TOP OF THE BASKET.
Prendre le dessus du panier.

"To take the cream of the crop." The French idiom pokes fun at the greengrocer's ancient and dishonorable custom of putting all the luscious berries on the top, and all the unripe or rotten ones underneath.

TO DRINK LIKE A HOLE.
Boire comme un trou.

"To drink like a fish." If you've ever dug a big hole to plant a bush, you'll

appreciate the French idiom. The hole
must be well watered before you plant
and the amount it can drink is
astonishing, puzzling, frightening.

TO GO DOWNSTREAM.
Aller à vau-l'eau.

This idiom refers to a business
enterprise and it means that it's "going
to the dogs." Our idiom is effective,
with hounds snapping and snarling over
someone's hard-earned bones. As for
aller à vau-l'eau, I see a small bistro or a
hat shop, rafting down a swift river,
heading toward the white-water rapids
just around the bend. *C'est la vie.*

TO RUN AFTER THE WIND.
Courir après le vent.

A foolish thing to do. It's like "going on
a wild-goose chase."

FRENCH IDIOMS
ABOUT FOREIGNERS

TO TAKE ENGLISH LEAVE.
Filer à l'anglaise.

The Italians also take "English leave,"
but the English, the Americans, and the

Spaniards all take "French leave." The term means unauthorized absence and evokes officers and gentlemen. Our term AWOL evokes fistfights with MPs in gin mills. "French leave" also means to leave a party without saying goodnight to the host or hostess.

TO ENGLISH SOMEONE.
Anglaiser quelqu'un.

"To fleece somebody." The French also use the verb *englander*. It sounds pretty and it means "to cheat."

IT'S CHINESE!
C'est du chinois!

That's funny, it's Greek to me! The Spaniards agree with the French, with their *¡Eso es chino para mi!* The Italians throw up their hands and say, "It's Arabic!" The French also use the phrase *C'est de l'algèbre!* and I know how they feel. All I know about algebra is that it comes from the Arabic word *al-jabr*, and means "the putting together of broken things."

TO DO THE GREEK.
Faire le grec.

To manipulate the cards. The French refer to professional card swindlers as "Greeks." In America, they were once called "cardsharps," and are now called "cardsharks." My gambling pals tell me that though these sharks are always skilled and ruthless players, they do not necessarily cheat.

TO BE STRONG AS A TURK.
Etre fort comme un Turc.

"To be strong as an ox." While admiring the Turk's strength, the French deplore his manners. *A la turque* (in the Turkish style) means "with rudeness." Speaking of rudeness, I might mention the well-known French expression "To speak French like a Spanish cow." It pretends to describe an atrocious French accent, but its main effect is to insult the Spaniard. A French acquaintance assures me that the original phrase was *parler français comme un Basque espagnol,* but since the Basques call themselves *vascos,* the French *vache* got lassoed into the saying. As I relate this Gallic explanation, I can see those Spanish eyes rolling.

It could be argued, feebly, that a bad accent hurts the French more than the rest of us because they care so deeply about their language. It's not surprising that our phrase is "Say it in plain English!" and their phrase is "Say it in good French!"

FRENCH IDIOMS ABOUT THE BODY, INSIDE AND OUT

TO LAUGH INTO YOUR BEARD.
Rire dans sa barbe.

> "To laugh up your sleeve." Ours is the better idiom. It conjures up a dreadful fop, stroking his mouth, snickering into his cuff.

TO MAKE YOUR MOUTH INTO A HEART.
Faire la bouche en coeur.

> This is adorable. It means "to play coy."

TO MAKE A LITTLE MOUTH.
Faire la petite bouche.

> If you make your mouth smaller by tightening your lips, your mien automatically becomes one of disapproval, just as if you were "turning up your nose."

MOUTH SEWN UP!
Bouche cousue!

> "Mum's the word!"

TO WALK ARM OVER, ARM UNDER.
Marcher bras dessus bras dessous.

> "To walk arm-in-arm." The finest practitioners of the art are the females in Spain. They begin to link arms with one another when they are six or seven years old and continue their arm-under, arm-over promenades for as long as they can walk.

TO HAVE A LOT OF CHILDREN ON YOUR ARMS.
Avoir beaucoup d'enfants sur les bras.

> We have a lot of children, too, but they are "on our hands."

TO SEIZE THE OPPORTUNITY BY THE HAIR.
Saisir l'occasion par les cheveux.

> "If you want to make hay while the sun shines, seize the bull by the horns."

TO CUT A HAIR IN FOUR.
Couper un cheveu en quatre.

>As a rule, we are less finicky than the French. "To split hairs" is as far as we'll go.

TO ARRIVE LIKE A HAIR IN THE SOUP.
Arriver comme un cheveu sur la soupe.

>To arrive at an awkward moment, or "to turn up like a bad penny."

THAT LIFTS MY HEART!
Ça soulève le coeur!

>This sounds as if the flag had just passed by, but what it means is "That turns my stomach!"

TO HAVE YOUR HEART ON YOUR LIPS.
Avoir le coeur sur les lèvres.

>"To wear your heart on your sleeve." If a Frenchman tells you that you have your heart in your hand, don't be uneasy. He's saying that you're a fine, big-hearted person. If he says you have an artichoke heart, he means that you fall for every pretty face that comes along, you devil.

TO HAVE A PAIN IN THE HEART.
Avoir mal au coeur.

>It's not as bad as it sounds. It means "to feel sick to your stomach."

IT'S NOT TO BE SPIT UPON.
Il ne faut pas cracher dessus.

> Our idiom should say the same thing, but we decided to be genteel. The result is "nothing to sneeze at."

TO TAKE THE MOON WITH YOUR TEETH.
Prendre la lune avec les dents.

> This is a glorious thought, but it represents an unattainable goal: what the ancient Greeks called an "eagle in the sky," and we call "pie in the sky."

TO HAVE A HARD TOOTH.
Avoir la dent dure.

> "To have a sharp tongue." The French make biting remarks. Our responses are cutting.

TO HAVE LIVERS.
Avoir les foies.

> The Frenchman worries a lot about his liver. The thought of having more than one is frightening. The idiom means "to have cold feet."

A BALL IN THE THROAT.
Une boule dans la gorge.

> Actually, it's more like a lump.

TO HAVE YOUR LEGS IN AN X.
Avoir les jambes en X.

> Their expression is visual. Ours is auditory: "to be knock-kneed."

TO HAVE A WELL-HUNG TONGUE.
Avoir la langue bien pendue.

To us, it's the "gift of gab." Gab is a grand word. Gab, gab, gab. It sounds like American slang, but its background is Nordic. It comes from the Icelandic verb *gabbern*, to mock. In Danish, *gab* means mouth.

TO MAKE A FUNNY NOSE.
Faire un drôle de nez.

To look disgruntled, "to pull a long face." If you stand in front of a mirror and try to do something funny with your nose, you'll see what the French are talking about.

FROM THE VIEW OF THE NOSE.
A vue de nez.

"By guess or by golly." "By rule of thumb."

HE LAUGHS IN YOUR NOSE.
Il vous rit au nez.

That's worse than "laughing in your face."

TO WARM SOMEBODY'S EARS.
Chauffer les oreilles de quelqu'un.

To chastise a person with such gusto that the blood rushes to his head, making his ears feel warm and look

pink. The angry American equivalent is
"to chew somebody out."

TO MAKE NEW SKIN.
Faire peau neuve.

> "I'm going to make new skin" sounds
> like a sincere promise to make a fresh
> start. "I'm going to turn over a new
> leaf" suggests a book whose pages will
> be turned again and again.

NOT TO KNOW WHICH FOOT TO DANCE ON.
Ne pas savoir sur quel pied danser.

> It's like being "all at sea." *Danser* takes
> part in two other glorious French
> expressions. "To dance in front of the
> buffet" means to go hungry. "We are
> dancing on a volcano" defines the
> human condition — past, present, future.

TO GET UP ON THE LEFT FOOT.
Se lever du pied gauche.

> "To get up on the wrong side of the bed"
> or "off on the wrong foot." Language
> presumes everyone should be right-
> handed, so the concept of left is gauche.
> The English word for "left" is Anglo-
> Saxon and originally it meant
> "worthless." We speak of a left-handed
> compliment, and we talk out of the left
> side of the mouth. The Spaniards
> sometimes use "left" to mean "crooked."

The Italian word for "left" says it all: It is *sinistra*.

TO CRY THUMB.
Crier pouce.

"To cry uncle." This American yelp signifying defeat harks back to Roman times.

SAVE YOUR SALIVA!
Epargne ta salive!

It means "Don't waste your breath!" but it means it more emphatically. Our idiom is more refined, but I like the snarl in the French one.

TO BREAK YOUR HEAD.
Se casser la tête.

"To rack your brains." The verb "to rack" means "to stretch mightily." From this comes the term "torture rack." A shelf for bric-a-brac and whatnots is also called a rack. Occasionally we go to rack and ruin. The word has not a single redeeming grace.

TO FALL FLAT ON YOUR STOMACH.
Tomber à plat ventre.

It means "to fall flat on your face" in the bodily sense. Ka-boom! When a French person falls flat on his back, the appropriate idiom is equine: *tomber les quatre fers en l'air* (to fall with four horseshoes in the air). Our verb "to fall" is Anglo-Saxon and sounds serious. Though it's possible for a Frenchman *tomber* to his death, the verb is so bouncy it implies a mere tumble.

FAR FROM EYES, FAR FROM HEART.
Loin des yeux, loin du coeur.

What ever happened to "Absence makes the heart grow fonder"? It's "out of sight, out of mind."

TO THROW POWDER IN YOUR EYES.
Jeter de la poudre aux yeux.

"To pull the wool over your eyes." We no longer wear woolen wigs that beg to be tweaked, but the saying lingers on.

FRENCH IDIOMS ABOUT SOCKS AND BUTTONS, DRESSES AND NIGHTCAPS

A WOOL SOCK, WELL-STUFFED.
Un bas de laine bien garni.

"A nice little nest egg." A nest egg, by the way, is one that is left in the nest to keep the laying hen from losing interest in her *raison d'être*.

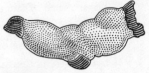

TO BE SAD AS A NIGHTCAP.
Etre triste comme un bonnet de nuit.

I'd never thought of a nightcap in that way. Perhaps it's all the wrinkles. The expression means "to be dreary" or "dull as ditchwater." A lot of people say "dishwater," which is dull enough, but the expression intends to contrast the placid water in a ditch with that of a babbling brook.

TO UNBUTTON YOURSELF.
Se déboutonner.

I love this one. It means, beyond the literal meaning, to relax and "let your hair down" and "speak your mind." *Se déboutonner* is not to be confused with *se débotter*, to de-boot yourself. *Au débotté* means "immediately upon arrival."

TO BE SEWN WITH GOLD.
Etre cousu d'or.

"To be filthy rich." The French phrase is all amazement and delight. Our phrase is sour grapes and spite.

ANOTHER PAIR OF SLEEVES.
Une autre paire de manches.

"A horse of a different color." Nobody

knows where the horse came from, but it's getting old. Shakespeare referred to a horse of the same color, making a nice twist on an obviously well-known expression.

IT'S IN THE POCKET!
C'est dans la poche!

Better yet, "it's in the bag!"

PUT THIS IN YOUR POCKET WITH YOUR HANDKERCHIEF ON TOP!
Mets-le dans ta poche avec ton mouchoir dessus!

It sounds like a complicated version of "Keep this under your hat," but it means "Put that in your pipe and smoke it!"

THAT TAKES THE POMPOM!
Ça c'est le pompon!

To us, "it takes the cake!" *Avoir le pompon* means "to have the upper hand."

AN ANIMAL WITH A BEAUTIFUL DRESS.
Un animal de belle robe.

We might say this about an organ-grinder's monkey, but that animal is usually wearing trousers and a little red fez. Referring to an animal's pelt, we say, "It has a beautiful coat."

FRENCH IDIOMS ABOUT BIRDS AND BEASTS, FISH AND INSECTS

THERE'S AN EEL UNDER THE ROCK!
Il y a anguille sous roche!

It means "I smell something fishy." The Spaniards also allude to a scent to express suspicion, but it comes from another critter: *Aqui hay gato encerrado* (Here we have a locked-up cat).

FOR THE LACK OF ONE POINT, MARTIN LOST HIS DONKEY.
Faute d'un point, Martin a perdu son âne.

Or, "A miss is as good as a mile." Martin was a saint, but he kept losing things. The Italians say, "By one point, Martin lost his cape." In the fourth century he left his cape or *cappa* at a little church in Tours, and that's the origin of the word *cappella,* or chapel. (So they say.) The best Martin saying comes from Portugal: "Every pig has his Martinmas." This sounds like "Every dog has his day," but what it means is "Every turkey has his Thanksgiving."

A SPIDER ON THE CEILING.
Une araignée au plafond.

I've seen "bee in the bonnet" listed as

the equivalent American idiom, but "bats in the belfry" is more like it. It's just as well that the French stick to spiders, for the language lacks a decent bat word. The people make do with *chauve-souris* (bald mouse), as if the remarkable difference between the animals were not the wings, but the amount of hair growing on their tiny bodies.

TO HAVE THE COCKROACH.
Avoir le cafard.

"To be down in the dumps." The French talk about the cockroach a lot. *Le cafard* defines the bug, but it also means a "squealer." There's an adjective *cafardeux*, that means "miserable," as in "I'm feeling a bit cockroach-ish today."

WHEN THE CAT'S AWAY, THE MICE DANCE.
Quand le chat n'est pa là, les souris dansent.

I move we outlaw all rhyming proverbs, beginning with "When the cat's away, the mice will play." The French version shimmers. Our version smirks.

TO CALL A CAT A CAT.
Appeler un chat un chat.

We "call a spade a spade." The idiom seems to demand brevity, and both the French and American versions are appropriately pithy. Still, there's

something to be said for the wordy version from Italy and Spain: "to call bread bread, and wine wine." Best of all, from the ancient Greeks: "to call figs figs, and a tub a tub."

TO BUY A CAT IN A POCKET.
Acheter chat en poche.

We "buy a pig in a poke." "Poke" is a funny Old Dutch word. It means "sack."

THERE ISN'T A CAT IN THE HOUSE!
Il n'y a pas un chat dans la maison!

We say, "There isn't a soul at home!" The Italians have the best version of this idiom: "I looked, but I didn't find a dog!"

TO HAVE OTHER CATS TO FLOG.
Avoir d'autres chats à fouetter.

From the cat's point of view, we are less cruel; we "have other fish to fry."

CAT'S WRITING.
Ecriture de chat.

Writing so illegible that it looks like "chicken scratches." Our idiom comes from the calligraphy that chickens

create by walking in the barnyard dust.
I can't imagine where the French idiom
comes from.

IT'S GOOD FOR THE DOGS!
C'est bon pour les chiens!

And it's good for nothing else. In other
words, "it's for the birds!"

A GOOD DOG NEVER GETS A GOOD BONE.
A bon chien, il ne vient jamais un bon os.

Or, "Nice guys finish last."

SHE'S AN OLD OWL.
C'est une vieille chouette.

If you ask us, "she's an old bat."

TO MAKE AN ELEPHANT OUT OF A FLY.
Faire d'une mouche un éléphant.

We prefer to make "a mountain out of a
molehill."

ONE SWALLOW DOESN'T MAKE A SPRING.
Une hirondelle ne fait pas le printemps.

In our neck of the woods, "one swallow
doesn't make a summer." It's the same
in Spain. This is a very old saying
(Cervantes quotes it in *Don Quixote*) and
there are other graceful variations:
"One flower doesn't make a garland,"
and "One flower doesn't make a
spring."

HE'S A FAMOUS RABBIT.
C'est un fameux lapin.

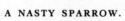

We think of him as a "sly devil." The rabbit also pops up in the French idiom *poser un lapin* (to break a date). If you want to break a date in Spain, you don't "pose a rabbit," you "do a monkey."

A NASTY SPARROW.
Un vilain moineau.

"An ugly customer." I don't know what the French have against the sparrow.

YOU COULD HAVE HEARD A FLY FLY.
On aurait entendu une mouche voler.

"You could have heard a pin drop" is how we'd put it. Idioms usually suffer in translation, but this one is enhanced. "Hearing a fly fly" not only delights the ear, it captures the essence of summer silence. Provence in August. Three in the afternoon.

TO SWALLOW THE FLY.
Gober la mouche.

We "swallow the bait." If we are especially gullible, we swallow it "hook, line, and sinker." Not all Frenchmen are fly-fishermen. There's another phrase, *gober le morceau* (to swallow the morsel), which must refer to whatever tidbit Monsieur has attached to the end of his line. (I went to a trout farm once and caught three trout with *morceaux* of some kind of fish mush.)

DON'T SELL THE BEARSKIN BEFORE YOU'VE KILLED THE BEAR.
Ne vendez pas la peau de l'ours avant de l'avoir tué.

Or, "Don't count your chickens before they have hatched." The French also use the phrase *un ours mal léché* (a disreputable bear) to describe an oaf. "Oaf" is such a satisfactory word we don't bother to use an idiom. The word is Icelandic and it used to mean "elf." How the wee elf turned into the big oaf is linguistic magic.

APRIL FISH.
Poisson d'avril.

A species of bass that is caught off the coast of Brittany in April, and is traditionally poached with prunes for the Easter feast. Ha, ha, April fool! The French, incidentally, don't play an April fool joke, they give someone an April fish.

TALL AS THREE APPLES.
Haut comme trois pommes.

I include this charmless French idiom, only because the American equivalent is so beguiling: "knee-high to a grasshopper."

POOR AS A CHURCH RAT.
Gueux comme un rat d'église.

An American is "poor as a church mouse." Actually, I think the two idioms mean the same thing, for the French use *rat* with abandon. They call wee, sleekit field mice *les rats des champs.*

CRAFTY AS A MONKEY.
Malin comme un singe.

This phrase describes a "sly fox," someone who's likely to "pull some monkey business."

TO PUT THE FLEA IN SOMEBODY'S EAR.
Mettre la puce à l'oreille à quelqu'un.

We are less particular. Any bug will do.

FRENCH IDIOMS ABOUT COLOR

A WHITE-BEAK.
Un blanc-bec.

"A greenhorn" or "rookie." The French also call a novice or an outsider a "blue." *Le bec* can mean the nose, the mouth, the lip, or the beak. *Avoir bon bec* is to be a good conversationalist. *Faire un bec à quelqu'un* is to give someone a peck on the cheek, although I never met a French person who was satisfied with one peck.

TO HAVE A BLUE FEAR.
Avoir une peur bleue.

"To be in a blue funk," "to be scared stiff."

TO SEE NOTHING BUT BLUE.
N'y voir que du bleu.

The blue refers to the sky, and the phrase means "to be left in the dark," usually in blissful ignorance.

TO BE IN A BLUE FURY.
Etre dans une colère bleue.

In other words, "a blind rage." The American idiom is powerful, but the French version is chilling. A red-faced man sputtering with rage is comical, but a man who's gone white — or palest blue — with fury? Beware.

A BLACK-BUTTER EYE.
Un oeil au beurre noir.

"A black eye." Black butter is a culinary term for butter that's more or less scorched. It's a very weird way to describe a bruise.

TO GRIND THE BLACK.
Broyer du noir.

It means "to be depressed," "to sing the blues." The musical term "blues," by the way, is now a genuine French word: *le blues.* So are *le rock 'n' roll* and *le jazz.* Pop music is sometimes called *le yéyé.* ("She loves yuh, yeh! yeh! yeh!")

A RED FISH.
Un poisson rouge.

We call it a "goldfish," with good reason. The creature in question is a carp that grows to a size appropriate to its watery environment. We put it in a little bowl and it remains small and gold. Given a pond, it grows into a spectacular *poisson rouge.*

A BLUE STORY.
Un conte bleu.

What sounds like an "off-color story" is quite the opposite: it's a "fairy tale." The origin of the word *bleu* or "blue" reveals a lot about the nature of the early human being. Though he lived

under the overpowering blue of the sky,
and sailed in vast blue seas, he named
the color for the mark that appeared on
his skin after he'd received a blow. The
French carry on the tradition by calling
bruises "blues."

TO SEE YELLOW.
Voir jaune.

"To look at things with a jaundiced eye."
(Note the French yellow in our
jaundice.) When a Frenchman is just
plain angry, he sees what we see: red.

TO SMILE YELLOW.
Rire jaune.

"To give a sickly grin." The Spaniards
describe this kind of smile with
perception: *reír con risa de conejo* (to
smile with a rabbit's smile). The caged
rabbit occasionally looks up from its
lettuce and twists its mouth into an
apologetic little smirk.

TO SEE EVERYTHING PINK.
Voir tout en rose.

"To look on the bright side," "to see the
world through rose-colored glasses."
Then there are those who tend to see
everything black: *voir tout en noir. A l'eau
de rose* (à la rose water) is the French
idiom for "sickly sweet."

TO HAVE A GREEN HAND.
Avoir la main verte.

>"To have a green thumb." This nation of green-handed gardeners creates beautiful gardens, but not always. In parts of Normandy, people edge their gardens with rocks painted white, and decorate their lawns with wooden ducks whose wings go 'round and 'round in the wind. Ugliness is rarely so neat.

FRENCH IDIOMS ABOUT FOOD AND KITCHENWARE

TO BE AN ASPARAGUS.
Etre une asperge.

>To be tall and lanky. A real "beanpole." A "string bean."

TO BE BUTTERED.
Etre beurré.

>"To be plastered." Buttered sounds better.

HE DIDN'T INVENT THE BUTTER CUTTER.
Il n'a pas inventé le fil à couper le beurre.

>In America, "he'll never set the world on fire." (The butter cutter is a length of

wire with which the French deftly cut butter and cheese.)

TO KEEP THE POT BOILING.
Faire bouillir la marmite.

"To bring home the bacon" or "earn the bread."

TO DRINK A CUP OF BROTH.
Boire un bouillon.

"Broth" symbolizes poor folks' fare. The idiom means "to go broke."

THE DAYS OF CHERRIES.
Les temps des cerises.

"The good old days." As Byron said, "All times, when old, are good."

IT'S CABBAGE GREEN AND GREEN CABBAGE.
C'est chou vert et vert chou.

"It's six of one, half a dozen of the other."

TO FATIGUE A SALAD.
Fatiguer la salade.

We prefer "to toss a salad." Our phrase must sound extraordinary to the French, as if we meant to hurl those greens across the room.

TO BE AN OIL.
Etre une huile.

> "To be a big shot."

KITCHEN LATIN.
Latin de cuisine.

> "Ig-pay atin-Lay."

IT'S GOOD AS BREAD.
C'est bon comme le pain.

> We obviously can't use our bread as a
> standard of excellence, so we resort to
> "good as gold." The Italians are justly
> proud of their bread: *è buono come il
> pane.* Bread in Spain is good, not great,
> and the Spanish version of the idiom
> admits the culinary truth: *Es más bueno
> que el pan* (It's better than bread).

TO BUY SOMETHING FOR A MOUTHFUL OF BREAD.
Acheter quelque chose pour une bouchée de pain.

> We "buy it for a song." This is a strange
> idiom for Americans to use. Arms
> folded, jaws clenched, we barely hum,
> much less sing out.

DEAF AS A POT.
Sourd comme un pot.

> We say "deaf as a post." Both idioms
> lack luster. The Italians say "deaf as a
> bell," as if the bell had gonged itself into
> a state of deafness.

TO TAKE A TURN AROUND THE POT.
Tourner autour du pot.

"To beat around the bush." Beating a bush with a stick makes the game birds fly into the air, so the hunter has a fair shot. It seems to me that beating *around* the bush would have the same effect on nervous quail, but evidently it doesn't.

TO PUT IN YOUR GRAIN OF SALT.
Mettre son grain de sel.

We "put our two cents in." Our contribution seems as paltry as a grain of salt.

TEMPEST IN A GLASS OF WATER.
Tempête dans un verre d'eau.

We create a "tempest in a teapot," and the French should, too, for our version of the proverb sounds rousing in French: *Une tempête dans une théière!*

FRENCH IDIOMS ABOUT NUMBERS

TO BREAK IN TWO.
Se casser en deux.

"To double up," "break up," "crack up,"

"split your sides." Lo, the violence of laughter.

TO WORK LIKE FOUR.
Travailler comme quatre.

It's what we all do: "work like mad," "like a beaver," "like a dog." The dog expression is puzzling. Hardworking sheep dogs, foxhounds, and circus poodles are surely not representative of dogdom.

TO BE ON FOUR PAWS.
Etre à quatre pattes.

What a wonderful phrase! It conjures up amiable prowling beasts and makes our idiom, "to be on all fours," seem very tame.

THE WEEK WITH FOUR THURSDAYS.
La semaine des quatre jeudis.

Never. "When hell freezes over." "When pigs have wings."

TO PUT ON YOUR THIRTY-ONE.
Se mettre sur son trente et un.

"To get dressed to the nines." Or even better, "To put your glad rags on."

TO SEE THIRTY-SIX CANDLES.
En voir trente-six chandelles.

"To see stars." It happens when someone "knocks the daylights out of you." This "daylights" phrase of ours is a beauty, but it doesn't mean what it says. The person whose daylights have been knocked out is staggering around and seeing stars, but he's not unconscious. Not to me, anyway.

SAY, "FORTY-FOUR!"
Dites, "Quarante-quatre!"

This is doctor talk. An American doctor says, "Say, 'Ah!'"

TO DO THE ONE HUNDRED STEPS.
Faire les cent pas.

It sounds like walking the last mile, but all it means is "to pace the floor."

TO STRIKE THE FOUR HUNDRED BLOWS.
Faire les quatre cent coups.

"To sow one's wild oats," or "to run wild," as a child. (In the title of the film *The 400 Blows*, Truffaut put this idiom to fine, bitter use.)

FRENCH IDIOMS ABOUT A CRACKED BELL, A PLETHORA OF SAINTS, ET CETERA

TO HAVE A CRACKED BELL.
Avoir le timbre fêlé.

"To be touched in the head" or "unhinged." The French have another colorful way to describe bizarre behavior: *yoyoter de la mansarde* (to yodel from the rooftop).

GOD'S FOOL.
La bête à bon Dieu.

We call it a "ladybug" or a "ladybird." (The lady in question is Our Lady, the Virgin Mary.) This small polka-dotted beetle is one of the world's best-loved bugs. In Spain, its true name is the *mariquita,* but it's also known as "Saint Anthony's Funnyface."

TO BE HOLDING UP LIKE THE PONT NEUF.
Se porter comme le Pont-Neuf.

The French use the image of this famous old bridge to say that an old duffer is "sound as a dollar."

TO BREAK YOUR PIPE.
Casser votre pipe.

"To kick the bucket." The French used to call the front lines the *casse-pipes.*

TO PERFORM ARIAS.
Faire des arias.

"To kick up a fuss."

TO PUT SOMEONE ON THE CHANDELIER.
Mettre quelqu'un sur le chandelier.

"To put someone in the limelight."

TO PLAY UNDER-FIFE.
Jouer en sous-fifre.

"To play second fiddle." The French turn
to fiddles for another idiom: *Il faut payer
les violons.* In America it's the piper who
must be paid.

NOT TO KNOW WHICH SAINT TO PRAY TO.
Ne savoir à quel saint se vouer.

"To be at the end of your tether." The
French idiom creates the picture of rose

windows and flickering candles, and a
row of marble saints inviting prayer.
Our idiom reminds me of some old goat
who's gone as far as he can go.

WHITE NIGHTS AND PERSIAN BLINDS AND OTHER ITALIAN INVENTIONS

Italian exuberance overwhelms me. Oh, the laughter, the jeers, the jokes, the gestures! The talent, the assurance, the curses, the praise! With an alphabet of twenty-one letters, the Italians have created a language that caresses and whines and bellows like no other. Eloquent voices are accompanied by a complex choreography of shrugging shoulders, tilting heads, and fluttering hands. Filled with admiration, and wary as a cat, I enter the world of Italian idioms.

To begin with, there is this noun: *dimenticatoio*. Its proper definition is "oblivion." But it also defines "an imaginary place to put forgotten things." A student, for example, has crammed for an examination. Six months later, he's forgotten all he knew. Is the knowledge lost? "No," says the Italian, "it's been placed in the *dimenticatoio*."

America lacks this Kingdom of Oblivion, but we do share other idioms with the Italians. We both talk about our old flames and our green thumbs. We agree that love is blind, and that it's useless to cry over spilt milk. Together we save face, lose face, and throw in the sponge. We both walk around with our heads in the clouds. We both know the meaning of hard times.

Some American and Italian idioms express the same thought in slightly different ways. In Italy, for example, steel wool is called *paglia di ferro* (iron straw). The statement below contains literal translations of several other Italian idioms. The style is odd, but the meaning is clear.

"I saw Johnny Niccolo in town this morning, and, as usual, he knocked me for money. You can imagine my reaction to this. Tomb silence! He said he's starting a new job next week, but I think he's lying through his throat. He still has charm, of course, and he never gives up. You must admit the fellow has liver. But as he walked off, I thought, 'Poor Johnny, he's lost his enamel.' "

Although Americans and Italians are close idiomatically, they don't always see eye-to-eye on the anatomy. An American is light-fingered. An Italian is swift of hand. An American does something behind your back, while an Italian does it behind your shoulders. We call each other blockheads. They call each other cabbage heads or turnip heads. A clumsy American is a butterfingers. A clumsy Italian has butter hands. And while an Italian never eats ladyfingers, he sometimes nibbles on cats' tongues.

Both Americans and Italians elbow their way through a crowd, but the Italians have a special idiom for "Make way!" It is *Fate ala!* (Make a wing!) This is a fine, terse way of saying, "Make a path through this crowd by walking swiftly with your hand on your hip!" An Italian, incidentally, doesn't take you under his wing, he takes you *sotto le ali,* or under his *wings,* a saying that reflects the broody-hen warmth of the Italian people.

Here's further evidence of the difference between the Anglo-Saxon and the Latin: an American says, "I believe it because I saw it with my own eyes!" An Italian says, "I believe it because I touched it with my hand!"

Every American speaks a little Italian. His vocabulary is limited but tasty: from *antipasto* to *spaghetti marinara* to *spu-*

mone, tortoni, or *zabaione.* Away from the dining table, the vocabulary dwindles down to *ciao* and *che sarà sarà.*

A few modern Italian words have become part of the American language. They make an odd but pretty collection, including: *ballerina, bordello, bravura, finale, incognito, replica, scenario,* and *studio. Belladonna,* the folk word for digitalis, means "beautiful lady" in Italian. The drug got this name because women once used it to dilate their pupils, for darker, more dazzling eyes. *Graffiti* comes from the verb *graffiare* (to scratch). The Italians have a saying that puts a graffiti artist in his place: *Muraglia bianca, carta di matto.* (A white wall is the fool's paper.)

Bimbo, an affectionate Italian word for "little boy," or "little kid," has entered our language, but lost its innocence. The word *confetti* also experienced a sea change. To an Italian, it means "sugar-coated almonds," often packaged in little boxes or fabric bags and handed out as party favors. Their word for our "confetti" is *coriandoli* (corianders). Another herb put to strange use in Italy is *finocchio,* or "fennel." It's slang for "homosexual."

Credenza, Italian for "faith," used to be the fancy American name for a sideboard, but the term seems to have gone the way of the davenport. This is just as well, since its background is sinister. The *credenza* used to be the table from which food was tasted before it was served to the king.

Our country bears an Italian name, and three other Italians roam throughout our language: Machiavelli, Casanova, and the physicist Alessandro Volta, who had the final vowel clipped from his name but lives on in the word "volt." To be electrically fair, the Italians call a watt a watt, in deference to James Watt, the Scottish inventor. This is no small concession, for the Italian alphabet lacks a *W.* Words beginning with this letter are all borrowed from other tongues. My Italian dictionary lists only these: *wafer, water-closet, watt, western, whisky* (no *e*), and *wigwam*. The letter *Y* gets even shorter shrift. It is represented by *yacht, yak, yankee,* and *yiddish.*

In America, a bad performance at an opera house receives a faint hiss and a boo or two. In an Italian opera house, unpleasing work is drowned out by the chorus of insults from the audience. This cry from the audience when a singer sings badly is called a *fiasco,* and the term has come to describe any theatrical disaster. Given this national passion for music, it's not surprising that the language of Western music is written in Italian.

Adagio is "slow," *scherzo* is a "joke," *largo* is "broad" or "ample." *Allegro* is "merry," *capriccio* is "whim," *piccolo* is "small," *piano* is "soft." (The instrument was originally named the "soft-loud," or *pianoforte.*) Musicians, of course, get their marching orders in Italian, from *affabile* (in a pleasing manner) to *zelosamente* (in an ardent and emphatic manner). The word *opera* means "work" in Italian. The world's first *Opera in Musica* was presented in Florence in 1597. Whether it was a *successo* or *fiasco* is unknown, since the score has been lost.

In Italy, all good singers are revered, and certain singers are eaten. These are the *beccafichi,* or "fig pickers," little song-birds that feed on grapes and figs. In France, the same delicacy is a *becfigue.*

By and large, the Italian language keeps to itself. Here are a few exceptions worth noting. "A peeping Tom" is called, in a tiny insult to the French, *un voyeur.* "A penny for your thoughts" becomes *un "penny" per sapere quello che pensi.* Sometimes the Italians borrow a phrase and promptly hack off the ending. Thus "nightclub" becomes *il night.* "Camping grounds" is *il camping.* "A bit of relaxation" is *un po' di relax.*

A few of our business and technical terms have captured

the fancy of the Italians: *il microchip, il minicomputer, il dischetto floppy, il knowhow.* They draw the line at "glut," preferring their own *sovrabbondanza* (overabundance). Their word is luscious, but I admire glut, and all the other push-and-shove words of American business: Ticker tape. Put and call. Break-even point. Slump.

One American conglomerate conducts a good deal of its business in Italian. Some of these Mafia terms have a ponderous dignity. The organization itself is called the "honored society." A brothel is called a "house of tolerance." The big boss is called "Mister sainted-mother." In the Sicilian dialect you'll find a presumptuous, a tomato, and an asparagus. A tough judge, a soft judge, and a prison guard, in that order. The company slogan, also in Sicilian, is a memorable one. It even rhymes.

> *Cu'e orbu, bordu e taci*
> *campa cent'anni 'n paci.*

> "He who is deaf, dumb, and blind
>   will live a hundred years in peace."

In passing, I offer this Sicilian nursery rhyme. It's comparable to "This little piggy," but it's played with the child's hand, beginning with the little finger.

> *Chistu voli pani,*
> *Chistu dici: 'Un cci nn'e,*
> *Chistu dici: Va 'rrobba,*
> *Chistu dici: 'Un sacciu la via,*
> *Chistu dici: Vicchiazzu, vicchiazzu,*
> *camina cu mia!*

> This one wants bread,
> This one says: "There isn't any."
> This one says: "Go and steal!"
> This one says: "I don't know the way."
> This one says: "Old man, old man,
> come with me!"

Although everyone agrees that the best Italian is from Tuscany, there's a famous old saying that recommends a *lingua toscana in bocca romana* (a Tuscan tongue in a Roman mouth). The phrase implies that northern speech, so cool and elegant, needs a dash of Roman wit and sass. All Italians, no matter what part of the country they come from, seem to talk very fast. Most of them don't, but it sounds that way because the language is heavily stressed and suffers from a *sovrabbondanza* of vowels. The language lacks the grandeur and power of terminal consonants. The idea expressed in "Forewarned is forearmed" loses something when it's trailing a string of vowels: *Uomo avvisato è mezzo salvato.*

Monosyllabic words are so rare that the following idiom seems to be written in another language. *In sè,* or "in self." (It means "to have yourself well in hand," the opposite of being "beside yourself.") Most of the time, the Italian rambles on at great length, to everyone's enjoyment. Here's a good example:

> *Quando nascono son tutti belli,*
> *Quando si maritano, tutti buoni,*
> *e quando muoiono, tutti santi.*

> When they are born, they are all beautiful,
> When they marry, they are all good,
> When they die, they are all saints.

Italian is not only phonetically pure, its vocabulary, compared to English, is extremely specific. Few words of any importance are burdened with more than one meaning. With one exception: *nipote.* It means granddaughter or niece or grandson or nephew. That four Italians of such national importance should be forced to huddle on one small substantive is astonishing. Look how the problem is solved in Latin:

nepos . . . . grandson
neptis . . . . granddaughter
fratris filius . . . . brother's son
sororis filius . . . . sister's son
fratris filia . . . . brother's daughter
sororis filia . . . . sister's daughter

That's one way to sort the children out.

An angry Italian sees red. A cowardly Italian is yellow. But when it comes to blue, Italians are strangely silent. An American sees you once in a blue moon. An Italian sees you every death of a pope. An American talks a blue streak, and eats blue cheese. An Italian talks like a rocket, and eats *gorgonzola americano.* Having the blues is a native American pastime. An Italian who is feeling bleak simply says he is "down in morale."

Both Americans and Italians build castles in Spain, but in other cases there is geographic disagreement. We go Dutch. They go Roman. We have Venetian blinds. They have Persian blinds. When an Italian wants to say "It's out of this world!" he says, "It's the end of the world!"

The language has its share of eccentricities. *Capezzolo,* the cozy word for "nipple," is a masculine noun. A sleepless night is described as a *notte bianca* (white night). Instead of saying "deep down," the Italian says *sotto sotto* (under under).

An Italian big shot is called a "fat dog" or a "big fish." An Italian mutt is called a "dog bastard," a term I find needlessly precise. To say something obvious in Italian is "to discover America." To go on a trip and gain nothing from the experience is *viaggiare come un baule* (to travel like a trunk).

Italians tend to look on the funny side. These are the people who call a chip on the shoulder a "fly on the nose." On the following pages you'll find examples of other merry Italian idioms. Yet there is another side to the language: austere, chilly, and as starkly beautiful as its Latin mother. Here are four such proverbs to ponder.

> *Breve orazione penetra.*
> Short prayers pierce.
>
> *Amor regge senza legge.*
> Love rules without rules.
>
> *Chi non fa, non falla.*
> He who does nothing, makes no mistakes.
>
> *Belle parole non pascon i gatti.*
> Fine words don't feed cats.

ITALIAN IDIOMS ABOUT THE COUNTRYSIDE

A TALL POPPY.
Un alto papavero.

Someone important. "A bigwig."

TO CATCH TWO PIGEONS WITH ONE BEAN.
Pigliare due piccioni con una fava.

The weapon under discussion is a dried legume. We use a stone, and any two birds serve as prey.

TO EAT LIKE A BUFFALO.
Mangiare come un bufalo.

"To eat like a pig." The Italian of boundless appetite also "eats with four jaws." Both Italians and Americans say that someone "eats like a horse," as if he or she subsisted on sweet grass and grain.

NAKED AS A WORM.
Nudo come un verme.

"Naked as a jaybird."

IN THE WOLF'S MOUTH!
In bocca al lupo!

> An Italian might say this to someone
> about to take an examination. It means
> "Good luck!" or "Go gettem, tiger!"

TO PLAY BLIND FLY.
Giocare a mosca cieca.

> "To play blindman's buff." *Buff* is a
> Middle English word for a "blow." The
> name of the game probably refers to the
> efforts of the blindfolded child to touch
> or strike the other players. Or "buff"
> could be the blindfold itself, for the
> word also means "softened buffalo
> hide." Or we could forget the whole
> thing and call it "blind fly."

BETTER A FINCH IN HAND THAN A THRUSH ON A BRANCH.
Meglio fringuello in man che tordo in frasca.

> The Italian version of "A bird in the
> hand. . . ." The thrush is more valuable
> because it's edible. The Italians also use
> the proverb *Meglio un uovo oggi che una
> gallina domani* (Better an egg today than
> a chicken tomorrow).

TO SLEEP LIKE A DORMOUSE.
Dormire come un ghiro.

> "To sleep like a top." The dormouse gets
> its name from the Latin *dormire* (to
> sleep) because it sleeps through most of
> the winter. We take note of its stillness

in our phrase "quiet as a dormouse." As for the "top" in our idiom, its employment as a symbol for deep slumber defies explanation, though a linguist once made this brave attempt: "When a top whirls at great speed, it appears to be motionless, as if it were 'asleep.' " Sure.

I collect fine definitions from dictionaries, and this one for "top" is one of my treasures:

Top. A child's toy, shaped like a pear, made to whirl on its point, by means of a string.

Look up the word when you get the chance. It's a pleasure to watch less gifted lexicologists get tangled up in their verbal strings. For example:

Top. A child's toy, shaped somewhat like an inverted cone, with a point at its apex upon which it is . . . [etc.]

TO SWALLOW THE TOAD.
Inghiottire il rospo.

"To eat crow."

DEAD NATURE.
Natura morta.

A "still life." A French still life is also called a "dead nature." The term came into use because pictures of this kind were so often strewn with slain game. To the Spaniards, a still life meant a painting of things to eat and drink: golden grapes and iridescent pheasants, wine in pewter tankards on rough-hewn tavern tables. They call this genre of painting a *bodegon* (literally, a saloon that serves food).

ITALIAN IDIOMS ABOUT KITCHENS AND FOOD AND DRINK

TO BE LIKE BREAD AND CHEESE.
Essere come pane e cacio.
"To be hand in glove" with someone.

TO HAVE THE KITCHEN SPOON IN HAND.
Avere il mestolo in mano.

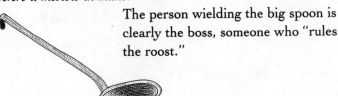

The person wielding the big spoon is clearly the boss, someone who "rules the roost."

TO EITHER DRINK OR DROWN.
O bere o affogare.

This is one of my all-time favorites, a great improvement over our solemn "sink or swim."

TO MAKE MEATBALLS OUT OF SOMEONE.
Fare polpette di qualcuno.

> "To mop the floor with someone" or
> "make mincemeat out of him."

CABBAGE!
Cavolo!

> "Rats!" (Cabbage can also be translated
> as a "blessed thing," as in "He didn't
> understand a cabbage!")

TO BE IN A LOVELY PIE.
Essere in un bel pasticcio.

> "To be in a pickle." Or worse, "to be in a
> fine pickle." The pie in the Italian idiom
> is usually made with meat. A pie made
> with fruit is a *torta.*

TO GIVE YOU THE BREAD FROM HIS MOUTH.
Togliersi il pane di bocca.

> "To give you the shirt off his back."

TO LOOK FOR HAIRS INSIDE AN EGG.
Cercare i peli nell'uovo.

> It's a dreadful thought, but so is our
> equivalent phrase: "to nitpick." And
> what about the slangy French version?

Enculer les mouches. It means — how shall I put it? — "to sodomize flies."

HE DRIVES AN OLD COFFEEPOT.
Guida una vecchia caffettiera.

We would call it a "rattletrap."

TO HAVE YOUR HANDS IN THE DOUGH.
Avere le mani in pasta.

"To be up on everything," "to know the ropes." An Italian who has his hands in the dough is also likely to "have his finger in every pie."

TO HAVE TOO MUCH MEAT ON THE FIRE.
Esserci troppa carne al fuoco.

This sounds like a barbecue that's gotten out of hand, but all it means is "to have too many irons in the fire." "Barbecue" is a nice word. I like the tricky spellings: "bar-b-que" and "bar-b-q." The word is close to the French *barbe-à-queue* (beard-to-tail), but it comes from the Caribbean *barbacoa*, which is a grill fashioned out of sticks and used for cooking meat.

SOMETHING'S BOILING IN THE POT.
Qualcosa bolle in pentola.

> Our culinary phrase is "Something's cooking." This something can also be "brewing," "up," "afoot," or "in the wind."

SPANISH BREAD.
Pane di Spagna.

> "Angel food cake." This cake for angels is fine, light, and colorless. Devil's food is better.

TOO MANY COOKS SPOIL THE DINNER.
Troppi cuochi guastano il pranzo.

> In America, a superfluity of cooks does nothing more than "spoil the broth." *Il pranzo* comes from the Latin *prandium*, the main meal of the day. In Italy, this main meal is often served at midday. (*Dopo pranzo*, "after the meal," is one way of saying "afternoon.") We ignore the noun *prandium*, but keep its Latin roots alive with the phrase "postprandial libation," a jocular way to describe an after-dinner drink that is usually green.

ITALIAN IDIOMS ABOUT CLOTHES

WITH YOUR HANDS IN YOUR BELT.
Con le mani alla cintola.

> Idling, loafing, "twiddling your thumbs."

TO DO IT BY THE RIP OF THE CAP.
Farcela per il rotto della cuffia.

> "To do it by the skin of your teeth," "to squeak through." The word *cuffia* is a shifty little noun. It means "cap," "baby's bonnet," "radio headset," and the "prompter's box at the theater."

TO PUT YOURSELF IN SOMEONE'S CLOTHES.
Mettersi nei panni di qualcuno.

> We feel it's sufficient "to put yourself in someone else's shoes."

TO HAVE PURSES UNDER THE EYES.
Avere le borse sotto gli occhi.

> In America they are "bags."

ITALIAN IDIOMS ABOUT
LIFE ON THE FARM

YOU'VE PUT THE CART BEFORE THE OXEN!
Hai messo il carro davanti ai buoi!

> No, "you've got the cart before the horse."

TO BREAK THE EGGS IN SOMEONE'S BASKET.
Rompere le uova nel paniere a qualcuno.

> To spoil someone's plans, "to rain on someone's parade." While we're on broken eggs, bear in mind that in Italy a scrambled egg is *uovo strapazzato* (a crumpled or bungled egg).

TO LEAD THE DOG THROUGH THE BARNYARD.
Menare il can per l'aia.

> "To beat around the bush." *Can* is literary Italian for "dog." The ordinary word is *cane*. It's used for the kind of actor we call a "ham." *Come un cane* (like a dog) means "all alone." There's a lovely phrase, *come un cane in chiesa* (like a dog in church) that means "an unwelcome guest."

TO GO HORSIE.
Andare a cavalluccio.

> "To ride pickaback." Small Americans who ride in this fashion have changed the word into "piggyback."

A DOG DOESN'T EAT A DOG.
Cane non mangia cane.

> "There is honor among thieves." Thieves aren't what they used to be. Honor is lost.

TO HAVE THE BRAIN OF A CHICKEN.
Avere il cervello di una gallina.

> "To be harebrained."

TO HAVE THE HEART OF A RABBIT.
Avere il cuore di un coniglio.

> "To be chickenhearted."

TO RACE THE YOUNG MARE.
Correre la cavallina.

> There's a beautiful canter in *correre la cavallina.* It expresses by sound as well as meaning the affectionate tolerance of an older person for the urgent needs of a younger one. It means "to sow your wild oats."

A BIG DOG.
Un cane grosso.

> "A big shot." A powerful Italian is also called *un pezzo grosso* (a big piece). *Un*

cane sciolto (a free dog) is a politician who doesn't align himself with others. He's a lone wolf, if not a dark horse.

PIG LEG.
Zampa di porco.

A "crowbar." The Italians use *porco* in the cranky little expletive *porco mondo!* (Pig world!)

IT'S A HARD BONE TO GNAW.
È un osso duro da rodere.

The Italian's attitude is dogged. Ours is squirrely: "It's a tough nut to crack."

ITALIAN IDIOMS ABOUT COLOR

TO BE AT THE GREEN.
Essere al verde.

"To be broke" or even "dead broke." Italians use *verdognolo* (greenish) to describe a sallow face.

TO TURN RED AS A PEPPER.
Diventare rosso come un peperone.

> "To turn red as a beet."

A YELLOW BOOK.
Un libro giallo.

> An Italian "whodunit."

A BLACK BOOK.
Un libro nero.

> "A blacklist."

A WHITE BOOK.
Un libro bianco.

> "A white paper."

A PINK NOVEL.
Un romanzo rosa.

> "A love story."

BLACK WORK.
Il lavoro nero.

> This sounds nefarious, but the black
> simply refers to the color of the sky.
> Our equivalent phrase is poetic:
> "moonlighting."

THE GREEN YEARS.
Gli anni verdi.

> The prime of life, or "heyday." "Hey" is
> Middle English for "high." I'm
> surprised and pleased that we use
> "heyday" in the singular, for it suggests

there is a high in each of our lives, just
one day when we are the best we'll
ever be.

GOLDEN DREAMS.
Sogni d'oro!

> "Sweet dreams!" "Sleep tight!"

ITALIAN IDIOMS ABOUT THE SEA AND THE CREATURES THEREIN

TO MOVE SEA AND MOUNTAINS.
Smuovere mare e monti.

> "To move heaven and earth." "To move"
> in Italian is usually just plain *muovere.*
> *Smuovere* means the same thing, but it
> adds a little "oof!" or "alley-oop!" to the
> action. Both verbs make lively
> imperatives. *Muoviti!* means "Hurry
> up!" *Smuoviti!* is more along the lines of
> "Move it, Buster!"

NOT TO KNOW WHICH FISH TO CATCH.
Non sapere che pesci pigliare.

> To be in a state of frantic indecision, "to
> not know which way to turn."

TO SWALLOW THE HOOK.
Abboccare all'amo.

> There's one born every minute. In Italy he swallows the hook. In France, he swallows the fly. In America, he swallows the story.

AN OLD SEA WOLF.
Un vecchio lupo di mare.

> "An old salt," or "a sea dog." The old Italian sea wolf, incidentally, doesn't have sea legs, he has *piedi di marinaro* (sailor's feet).

HE WHO SLEEPS CATCHES NO FISH.
Chi dorme, non piglia pesci.

> We chide our layabouts with a different phrase: "The early bird catches the worm." What the snoozing Italian fails to catch are *pesci,* which should be translated as "fishes." For some reason, we rarely use the plural form for fish, sheep, elk, or for any of the animals in "Home on the Range." I've been trying to decide if we ever use the plural for moose. I don't think so. "How many mooses did you bag?" doesn't sound right.

AN ARK OF SCIENCE.
Un'arca di scienza.

> "A walking encyclopedia."

IT'S A DROP IN THE SEA.
È una goccia nel mare.

> We don't minimize a contribution to the Italian extent. To us, "it's a drop in the bucket."

HEALTHY AS A FISH.
Sano come un pesce.

> "Sound as a dollar," or "sound as a bell." In English we've made a real mess out of "sound" by lumping together the Latin words *sanus* (healthy) and *sonus* (noise). To make things interesting, we also assign the word to a large body of water. Then there's the verb. It means "to seem," "to make noise," and "to measure the depth of water." Ponder the possibilities. Such as:
>> "I hear they're going to sound the sound. Does that sound sound to you?"
>
> The air bladder of a fish is also called a "sound," but don't spread it around.

ITALIAN IDIOMS ABOUT HEARTS AND OTHER PARTS

TO HAVE LIVER.
Avere fegato.

It means "to have courage." When we want to use innards to express this quality, we talk about "guts." I just looked up "guts," to my regret. The term "entrails" is acceptable, but I'd rather not contemplate "the intestinal canal of an animal from the stomach to the anus." What a strange symbol for valor. Returning to the Italian liver for a moment, I should mention *rodersi il fegato* (to gnaw on one's liver). It means "to seethe with rage." The Spaniards use the liver to communicate bravery, and it's always in the plural: *tener higados* (to have livers). The French use the same phrase, *avoir les foies*, but in their case it means "to be scared stiff."

The Americans never play word games with their livers, but they bandy other bodily parts about:

"I've been eating my heart out about this for months. Now I've got to get it off my chest. I've had a bellyful of your lying ways and can't stomach you a moment longer. You are nosy,

cheeky, heartless, spineless, and a
royal pain in the ass!"

TO BE ON THE LEG.
Essere in gamba.

"To be on your toes" or "on the ball."
Italians use their legs to good advantage
in another idiom: *a gambe all'aria* (legs
in the air). It means "upside down."

PRIDE RODE OUT ON HORSEBACK AND CAME BACK ON FOOT.
La superbia andò a cavallo e tornò a piedi.

"Pride goeth before a fall."

TO BATHE YOUR THROAT.
Bagnarsi la gola.

The Italian idiom is adequate. Ours is a
festive little poem: "to wet your
whistle."

TO DROP YOUR ARMS.
Cascare le braccia.

An Italian with his arms hanging quietly
at his sides? This describes a person
who has "lost heart."

DON'T LOSE YOUR HAIR!
Non perdere i capelli!

"Keep your temper!" "Don't lose your
cool!"

TO GIVE SOMEONE A HEAD WASHING.
Dare una lavata di capo a qualcuno.

> Head washing sounds harmless, but it
> hurts. We call it a "tongue lashing."

A FRIEND OF THE HEART.
Un amico del cuore.

> "A bosom friend." Italians also talk
> about *un amico per la pelle* (a friend
> through the skin), someone who stands
> by you through thick and thin. *Stringere
> amicizia con* means "to make friends
> with." I cherish the endeavor, but their
> verb makes me nervous: *stringere* (to
> tighten, press, clinch, or grip).

A MOUTHFUL OF AIR.
Una boccata d'aria.

> "A breath of fresh air." The Italian
> phrase is a beauty, evoking air so cool
> and sweet it must be gobbled.

TO LIE THROUGH THE THROAT.
Mentire per la gola.

> "To lie through the teeth."

WITH GOOD BELLY.
Di buzzo buono.

> Willingly, wholeheartedly, usually in
> "dead earnest."

TO LICK THE FINGERS.
Leccarsi le dita.

> The finger licking is done in anticipation
> of pleasure, for the phrase describes the
> euphoria brought on by the sight of
> delectable food. We don't lick our
> fingers, but we "smack our lips" and
> sometimes lapse into baby talk:
> *yum yum!*

TO PUT YOUR HEART AT PEACE.
Mettersi il cuore in pace.

> We say, "to set your mind at rest." The
> two phrases mean the same thing, but
> "a heart at peace" is the far grander
> notion.

TO HAVE A FLY ON YOUR NOSE.
Avere la mosca al naso.

> "To have a chip on your shoulder." No
> one knows much about this chip, but
> we've been grousing about it for more
> than a hundred years. Imaginative
> linguists hazard the guess that once
> there was a real chip of wood, resting
> on the shoulder of a truculent
> woodsman who dared anyone to knock
> it off. I'll buy that.

DON'T TAKE A STEP LONGER THAN YOUR LEG.
Non fare il passo più lungo della gamba.

> "Don't bite off more than you can chew."

TO CURVE YOUR BACK.
Curvare la schiena.

> This one tickles me. It means "to lower your sights." Picture the hunter all bent out of shape trying to take aim at his prey.

ITALIAN IDIOMS ABOUT THE CHURCH AND HIS HOLINESS

EVERY DEATH OF A POPE.
Ad ogni morte di papa.

> Rarely, if ever. "Once in a blue moon." The Italians are nonchalant about their accent marks, but in the case of *papa,* the rule is strict. *Mamma e Papa* means "Mummy and the Pope." "Daddy" is *papà.*

TO LIGHT A CANDLE.
Accendere una candela.

> "To thank your lucky stars." The Italians are Catholic, and we appear to be pagan.

TO RIDE ON SAINT FRANCIS'S HORSE.
Andare col cavallo di San Francesco.

> To walk. "To ride on shank's mare."
> Saint Francis, you may remember, was
> born rich. When he entered religious
> life, he gave away all his worldly
> possessions, including his stables.

HAPPY AS EASTER.
Felice come una Pasqua.

> "Happy as a lark, "bubbling with joy,"
> "tickled pink." The Italian word for
> Easter or Passover comes from the
> Hebrew word *pesach*. In France, it's
> *Pâques*. In Spain, *Pascua* means
> Passover, or any of the Catholic
> holidays. For Easter, the word wears
> flowers: *Pascua florida*.

AN ANGEL DIVE.
Un tuffo ad angelo.

> We call it "a swan dive." The Italians
> also use *volo dell'angelo* (angel's flight) to
> describe this aquatic feat. In both
> languages the dive is compared to an
> image seen only in the mind's eye, since
> diving swans are almost as rare as
> plunging angels. The swans I know
> glide serenely on glassy bays, imitating
> the art of John Milton's swan who
> "rows her state on oary feet." All our
> local swan dives are idiomatic.
>   The legend of the swan who began to

sing just before the moment of death caught the fancy of the ancient Greeks and everyone ever after. The result is a beautiful idiom, no matter which language: swan song, *canto del cigno*, *chant du cygne*, *Schwanengesang* . . .

TO UNVEIL LITTLE ALTARS.
Scoprire gli altarini.

"To let the cat out of the bag."

TO BE LIKE A POPE.
Stare come un papa.

It doesn't mean to be holy, it means to be rich, "to live like a king."

ITALIAN IDIOMS ABOUT FELLOW ITALIANS AND THE TURKS

TIZIO, CAIO, E SEMPRONIO.

"Tom, Dick, and Harry."

TO GO ROMAN.
Fare alla romana.

"To go Dutch." A "Dutch treat" is called an *invito alla romana* (a Roman invitation). The Italians, by the way, display a curious attitude toward the Dutchman by calling him a *tedesco*, or

"German." (The proper word is *olandese*.) But who are we to talk? We've always called the Pennsylvania Germans "Dutch."

TO LEAD THE LIFE OF MICHELACCIO.
Fare la vita di Michelaccio.
> "To lead the life of Riley."

TO SWEAR LIKE A TURK.
Bestemmiare come un turco.
> "To swear a blue streak."

TO DRINK LIKE A TURK.
Bere come un turco.
> "To drink like a fish."

TO SMOKE LIKE A TURK.
Fumare come un turco.
> "To smoke like a chimney."

TO SIT LIKE A TURK.
Sedere alla turca.
> "To sit cross-legged." That completes the Italian's portrait of the Turk: a gentleman sitting cross-legged on the floor, with a cigarette in one hand, a drink in the other, and a blue streak coming from his mouth.

ITALIAN IDIOMS ABOUT CRIME, DEATH, AND MISCELLANEOUS MISFORTUNES

THEY'VE SENT OFF THE BOMB!
È scoppiata la bomba!

> Though the phrase seems to herald Doomsday, the meaning is less spectacular. In other words, "the fat's in the fire!"

TO SHOOT OFF YOUR LAST CARTRIDGE.
Sparare l'ultima cartuccia.

> This sounds even more desperate than "playing your last card." In Italy, cards come up in the proverb *È meglio non puntare tutto su una carta sola* (It's best not to bet everything on a single card). The cards in question could be *carte francesi,* which are the kind we play with, or *carte napoletane,* with suits of clubs, cups, swords, and gold coins.

TO MAKE A DROP-DEAD.
Fare il cascamorto.

> "To make sheep's eyes." *Il cascamorto* (the drop-dead) is a word used for a languishing lover, someone who is mooning around because he or she is lovesick.

TO LEAVE THE HINGES.
Uscire dai gangheri.

> "To fly off the handle." The verb *uscire* implies escape, so the idiom describes a kind of freedom from the hinges of propriety. *Uscire di senno* (to escape from wisdom) is "to go mad."

HE'S REDUCED TO A RAG.
È ridotto a un cencio.

> The poor fellow is a "shadow of his former self."

TO BREAK YOUR HORNS.
Rompersi le corna.

> "To run into a brick wall." *Fare le corna* (to make horns) is to wish someone evil by the gesture of your hand. (If you'd like to try it, tuck your thumb and two middle fingers into your palm. Now with a stiff arm, point your devil's horns at your enemy.) The phrase also means "to cuckold someone." "To have someone on your horns" means you dislike him a lot.

TO FIND YOURSELF ON THE PAVEMENT.
Trovarsi sul lastrico.

> "To be in the poorhouse." The Italian idiom describes simple poverty. The American phrases, "on the pavement," or "in the gutter," are usually reserved

for those who are not only poor, but
drunk, drugged, or mad.

TO LOSE THE NORTH WIND.
Perdere la tramontana.

> To be in a dither, to "not know whether
> you're coming or going." Sometimes it
> means a more serious state, "to go off
> your rocker." The graceful word
> *tramontana* is literally "between the
> mountains," which is the path the north
> wind takes as it sweeps down the Italian
> peninsula.

YOUR DEATH, MY LIFE.
Morte tua, vita mia.

> "One man's meat is another man's
> poison."

TO CATCH SOMEONE WITH HIS HANDS IN THE BAG.
Prendere qualcuno con le mani nel sacco.

> "To catch someone red-handed."

TO LOSE THE LIGHT OF REASON.
Perdere il lume della ragione.

> "To fly into a rage." The Italian idiom is
> cooly intellectual. The American phrase
> is more disturbing — airborne fury with
> a sharp beak and flapping wings.

BY LOVE OR BY FORCE.
Per amore o per forza.

> "By hook or by crook," or "willy-nilly."

Nil, the Latin word for "nothing," is part of our vocabulary. *Nill* isn't. The roots of this word are Anglo-Saxon, and it means "not to will." Shakespeare used it deftly thus: "and will you, nill you, I will marry you." This handsome verb has fallen upon hard times, but it still lives, willy-nilly, in our language. As for *per amore o per forza*, the Italians revel in the rhythm of this phrase, and have invented several others that swing along in the same way: "by good or bad," "straight or backwards." Their finest effort is *di riffa o di raffa* (by lottery or by violence). Even though our riffraff goes in for gambling and violence, the American word has nothing to do with *riffa-raffa*.

ITALIAN IDIOMS ABOUT A LITTLE LANTERN, AN INFLATED BALLOON, ET CETERA

WITH HIS TRUMPETS IN A BAG.
Con le trombe nel sacco.

The idiom describes a musician who's been asked not to play. It means "crestfallen." The Italians also make use of the rooster's crest. "To lower the

crest" is "to yield." "To raise the crest"
is "to become cocky."

WHEN AT A DANCE, ONE MUST DANCE.
Quando si è in ballo, bisogna ballare.

"In for a penny, in for a pound."

TO GIVE SOMEONE A BLANK DOCUMENT.
Dare carta bianca a qualcuno.

"To give someone a free hand."
Originally, this blank document was
signed, giving the bearer the freedom to
write his own demands. The French call
it *carte blanche* and so do we.

TO LOOK WITH A LITTLE LANTERN.
Cercare col lanternino.

"To look high and low." Our search
sounds brisk and efficient, but the
Italian search is doomed, with that tiny
lanternino flickering in the darkness.

THE MAN OF THE DAY.
L'uomo del giorno.

Fame in America is briefer still. We
speak of "the man of the hour."

TO HAVE THE LANGUAGE OF A PORTER.
Avere un linguaggio da facchino.

"To swear like a trooper." To understand
why a porter swears, you have to learn
another idiom: *lavore come un facchino.* It
means "to work like a slave."

TO CHANGE SOMEONE'S PERSONAL CHARACTERISTICS.
Cambiare i connotati a qualcuno.

> This phrase has a fine Pygmalion ring,
> but what does it mean? "To beat
> someone to a pulp."

TO MOUNT A DESK.
Montare in cattedra.

> "To pull rank," or "to get on your high
> horse." *Una cattedra* is a teacher's desk,
> or a professorship or chair at a
> university. The word has charming
> origins. It's from *kathedra* (literally, a
> "sit down"), which is ancient Greek for
> a "bench." We use the word in its Latin
> form, *cathedra*. It's the proper term for a
> bishop's chair, which is of course in the
> cathedral. *Ex cathedra* means "with
> official authority."

TO GO BY HICCUPS.
Andare a singhiozzo.

> "To go by fits and starts."

UGLY AS HUNGER.
Brutto come la fame.

> "Ugly as sin." Their idiom expresses a
> brutal truth. Ours means well, but it's
> holier-than-thou.

THE LESS COMPANY, THE MORE PEACEFUL LIFE.
Poco brigata, vita beata.

> I doubt that many Italians take this
> saying seriously. In Italy, the more

brigata, the merrier. Our closest equivalent is the old taunt hurled at the luckless person in the company of a couple bent on romance. The Italians should adopt our "Two's company, three's a crowd." It has its uses, and it sounds terrific: *Due fanno compagnia, tre fanno folla.*

TO HANDLE WITH PLIERS.
Prendere con le pinze.

"To handle with kid gloves."

ON THE OTHER SONG.
D'altro canto.

It's a charming phrase. "On the other hand," it's altogether too charming. Fortunately, an Italian who wishes to quibble has other choices: *d'altro lato* (on the other side) and *d'altra parte* (on the other part).

NOT WORTH AN H.
Non vale un'acca.

"Not worth a damn," "a straw," or "a fig." (Imagine the days of sweet purple figs, when they grew in such abundance they seemed worthless.) As for the Italian H, it's a member of the Italian alphabet, but beyond *hurra, hollywoodiano,* and *hockeista* (hockey player), it isn't worth a hoot.

UNDER UNDER.
Sotto sotto.

"Deep down." Italians frequently repeat words to make a point. *Attorno attorno* (around around) means "here, there, and everywhere." *In fretta in fretta* (in haste in haste) means "a mad dash." *Pelle pelle* (skin skin) means "skin deep." Repeating words in English doesn't get you very far. Bye-bye. Boo-boo. So-so. Too too. Ta-ta. It's the prattle of toddlers.

AN INFLATED BALLOON.
Un pallone gonfiato.

"A stuffed shirt." "Stuffy," for short.

TO BE ON HOT COALS.
Essere sui carboni ardenti.

"To be on pins and needles," which is a good sharp image, or "to be on tenterhooks," which is blurry. (A tenter is a rack for stretching cloth.)

TO LET (THINGS) RUN.
Lasciar correre.

"To let things slide." Behold the great difference between the Italian world

and our own. Things left unattended in
Italy continue to run. If American
things are left unattended they start
going downhill. No wonder we don't sit
around in sidewalk cafés.

FUROR IN A SEPIA ATRIUM AND OTHER LATIN IMAGES

Though the Latin language is dead and gone, there are those who refuse to give up the ghost. All over the world, in sweet, secret defiance of the Second Vatican Council, small groups of Catholics celebrate Mass in Latin. In a school not far from my village, sixth-grade students give plays in Latin, trailing around in togas, lolling on pillows on the floor, and serving, at the interval, Roman refreshments of fish hash and honey cakes. Over in Rome, a Catholic priest, the Reverend Lamberto Pigini, started a Latin comic book in 1982. A year later, he had 200,000 subscribers in England, Germany, France, and Italy. I haven't heard lately how he's doing, but I wish him well.

The language is far too exciting to abandon. I, for one, ignore the declensions and the Punic Wars and concentrate on the poetry, the proverbs, and words like *aqua limonata* (lemonade), *latebricola* (a person who hangs around dives and brothels), and *muscarium* (fly swatter). I should mention that the *muscarium* was made of peacock feathers. You didn't kill flies with it, you just wafted them away.

The greatest pleasure of all is to sift through old Latin epigrams and maxims. They are not only witty and wise, but often at odds with each other. Here's Statius speaking solemnly: "Take time for deliberation. Haste spoils everything." Hot on his heels comes Quintilian, bleating, "While we deliberate about beginning, it is already too late to begin!"

Compare Cicero's prim words: "The comfort derived from the misery of others is slight," to the exuberant malice in Lucretius's line: "It is pleasant, when the sea runs high, to view from the land the great distress of another."

In this case, the truth lies somewhere in the middle, and wasn't properly expressed until Alexander Pope came along: "I never knew any man in my life who could not bear another's misfortunes perfectly like a Christian."

Pope said something else that's made me stop and think:

> Authors, like coins, grow dear as they grow old;
> It is the rust we value, not the gold.

Is it the age of these Latin adages that makes them seem particularly precious? I don't know. The words are splendid, but the fact that they come crashing through the boundaries of time, century after century, to arrive safe and sound in our era, certainly adds to the excitement.

If you were lucky enough to be mentioned by name in an old Roman saying, you achieved a strange immortality. Davus, for instance. He lives on in the phrase *Davus sum non Oedipus* ("I am Davus, not Oedipus"), which means "I'm no good at riddles." *Consule Planco* (when Plancus was consul) means "when I was a young fellow." Then there's Belisarius, a general under Emperor Justinian who was neglected by the state and forced to beg in his old age. His plight inspired the words *Data obolum Belisario* (Give a coin to Belisarius). The phrase is a plea for charity toward all public servants who have fallen on hard times.

Finally, there's Crispus, in his lifetime the most boring man in Rome. He is immortalized in the phrase "Here comes that fellow Crispus," which means "A terrible bore is headed in our direction." Don't ask for the phrase in the original Latin. I lost it. Since it's the only reference card I lost while writing this book, I feel lucky. Look what happened to Eugene Ehrlich, author of the fine contemporary book on Latin *Amo, Amas, Amat, and More*. On the Acknowledgments page he thanks the gentleman who taught him how to use the IBM Personal Computer.

> . . . so that an ancient language could be treated, perhaps for the first time ever, within the confines of a cathode ray tube. Only once did his ministrations fail to rescue me from the effects of my computer illiteracy: At one time I lost an entire section of the book somewhere within the computer memory, and for all I know, it is lurking there to this day.

Words originally incised in wax, trapped inside a recalcitrant machine. It's an entrancing thought.

The best of the Roman epigrams and maxims apply to Everyman of All Times. Even so, it's intriguing to think of them as the *bon mots* of their day, and to imagine how they sounded when first spoken. That's my only excuse for the following play on words.

CICERO'S DINNER PARTY

Juvenal took a dainty sip of his mineral water and said, pointedly, "Our prayers should be for a sound mind in a healthy body." Phaedrus, paying no attention, helped himself to a third piece of cake, and beckoned to the servant for more wine.

Cicero smiled politely at his greedy houseguest, who was beginning to get on his nerves, and said, "He's right, my dear Phaedrus. You should eat to live, not live to eat. Remember, as you sow so shall you reap." With that, he leaned over and poked Phaedrus in the belly, a little harder than he intended. Phaedrus, startled, spilled wine all over his new toga. In a fury, he shouted at Cicero, "What will you do to yourself, now that you've added insult to injury?" Then he stormed out of the room.

Cicero turned to his other guests and heaved a sigh. "Well, we've managed to have another quarrel. Sometimes I fear man is his own worst enemy."

"Nonsense," said Plautus, "no one can be so welcome a guest that he will not become an annoyance when he has stayed in a friend's house for three continuous days."

"He's been here a week," said Cicero. Everybody moaned. "He's supposed to stay until the end of the month. I *can't* ask him to leave."

Old Publilius Syrus leaned over and patted Cicero on the shoulder. "My boy, no one knows what he can do until he tries."

The greatest writer of the proverbs and maxims of any language is Anonymous, but a surprising number of old Latin phrases arrive in our midst with neat little name tags. The trouble is, the tags are sometimes misleading. The phrase *Habent sua fata libelli* (Books have their own destiny) is the only fragment that remains of the poetry of Terentius Maurus. It's not fair that the line is usually attributed to Horace. *Ars longa, vita brevis* (Art is long, life short) is usually listed as a Latin maxim. Indeed it was. But the original thought is Greek. Hippocrates expressed it in 400 B.C.

The French lay claim to *Il n'est sauce que d'appétit* (There's no sauce like appetite). Dig deeper, and you'll find it in medieval Latin: *Fames est optimus coquus* (Hunger is the best cook). Long before that, in Greece, Xenophon said, "There's no condiment like appetite." Cicero put it another way: "I hear Socrates saying that the best seasoning for food is hunger; for drink, thirst."

The ancient Romans had a ready response to this sort of persnickety probing into authorship:

Pereant qui ante nos nostra dixerunt.

Freely translated this means: "To hell with those who said our good words before us!"

Americans have ceased to study Latin, but they continue to sprinkle it, like salt, on the English language.

> Ad hoc. Vice versa. Ex post facto. Ipso facto. Status quo. Alter ego. Bona fide. Quo vadis? Alma mater. Ante bellum. Deus ex machina. Prima facie. Tempus fugit. Habeas corpus. Mea culpa. Post partum. Post mortem. Per annum. Per capita. Per diem. Per se. Circa. Magna cum laude. Emeritus. Interim. Non sequitur. Non compos mentis. E pluribus unum. Ad infinitum. Ad absurdum. Ad nauseam.
>
> FINIS

We're on friendly terms with all these Latin words, but we've never embraced them fully. They're fine, but a little fancy, in the same league as "nuance" and "naïveté." Other Latin words, however, have slipped into the language and wander around at will, with no academic overtones, no togas. For instance: Furor. Sepia. Atrium. Creator. Odor. Consensus.

Administrator. Appendix. September. October. November. December.

Occasionally, we pick up a Latin word and give it a different meaning. *Obnoxius* in Latin is "culpable." *Disco* is "I learn."

Sometimes, we use abbreviations for Latin phrases, although I wish we wouldn't. I've no objection to A.M. and P.M. and A.D. It's viz. and etc. and i.e. and e.g. that I hate. Little bristly things. And what about M.A. and B.A. and M.O. and P.S.? This distressing habit dogs us till the end of our days, when we lie beneath an abbreviated blessing: R.I.P.

Latin not only inhabits the vocabularies of our legal, medical, and pharmaceutical professions, it pops up out in the garden, thanks to Carolus Linnaeus. He was the eighteenth-century Swedish botanist who devised the binominal classification of animals and plants, and even the humblest of wild flowers were caught in his linguistic net. Each plant was christened with two names. The first, for the genus, is usually Greek. The second name, for the species, is usually Latin. A hollyhock is known as *Althea rosea* all over the world, for Linnaeus's language is the Esperanto of the planet's gardeners.

Latin, which turned out to be so concise and refined, was born in the fifth century B.C. as a rough and rowdy tongue of the farmer-warriors who lived at the mouth of the Tiber. In four hundred years it was in full flower, with Virgil's *Aeneid* the testimony to its grace and power. Even when the empire that forged the language crumbled and disappeared, Latin hung on, though the common folk were chipping at its foundations. Grammarians of the era fought the changes, as they always do, but change was in the wind. By the ninth century, the French language was born, followed a century later by Spanish and Italian.

These three Roman or "Romance" languages are represented earlier in this book by collections of their idioms and proverbs. On the following pages, a few words from the matriarch.

Latin has never been shy. It leaps up and grabs you, if not by the throat, by the lapels. It seems to have been born with the ability. One of the earliest written records we have of the language is from 500 B.C. Just four words, engraved on a belt buckle:

Manios med fhefhaked Numasioi
Manius made me for Nummerius

LATIN IDIOMS ABOUT ANIMALS AND BIRDS AND BEES

HE HAS HAY ON HIS HORN, BEWARE OF HIM.
Faenum habet in cornu, longe fuge.

> The Romans were wary of bulls who gored haystacks. The proverb warns against the man who exhibits taurine traits.

HE QUARRELS OVER GOAT'S HAIR.
Rixatur de lana caprina.

> "He quibbles over straws." Fabric woven of wool was prized, fabric woven of goat's hair wasn't.

A RARE BIRD UPON THE EARTH AND VERY LIKE A BLACK SWAN.
Rara avis in terris nigroque simillima cycno.

To the Romans, a black swan was an anomaly, as impossible as a white crow. It's just as well we've shortened the line to *rara avis.*

BEWARE OF THE SILENT DOG AND STILL WATER.
Cave tibi cane muto, aqua silente.

Stagnant water can poison you. Silent dogs can bite. Taciturn adversaries are more dangerous than the ones who whoop and holler.

A BLACKBIRD ALWAYS SITS CLOSE TO A BLACKBIRD.
Semper graculus assidet graculo.

Birds of a feather sit close together.

THE LION DIES AND EVEN THE HARES INSULT HIM.
Mortuo leoni et lepores insultant.

Here's evidence that the Romans didn't always abide by their famous tenet, *De mortuis nil nisi bonum* (Let nothing but good be said of the dead).

A HAPPY MAN IS RARER THAN A WHITE CROW.
Felix ille tamen corvo quoque rarior albo.

> The happy-go-lucky word *felix* fared
> well as it pranced into Spanish *(feliz)*
> and French *(félicité)*, but it sure came a
> cropper in English: felicitations,
> felicitous, felicitously.

O HAWK, THE DOVE THAT'S BEEN WOUNDED BY YOUR
TALONS IS FRIGHTENED BY THE LEAST FLUTTER OF A
FEATHER.
Terretur minimo pennae stridore columba
Unguibus, accipiter, saucia facta tuis.

> The French, Italian, and Spanish have
> turned Ovid's high-flown phrase into
> something more prosaic: "A scalded cat
> is afraid of cold water." To express the
> same thought proverbially, we would
> have to say, "A burned child is afraid of
> a puff of smoke."

EVEN A FLY HAS A SPLEEN.
Habet et musca splenem.

> The Romans believed that anger was
> housed in the spleen, and we still cling
> idiomatically to the thought. Our
> translation of this saying is "The worm
> turns." In France and Spain, "the ant
> has its ire." In Italy "even the fly has its
> fury." The strangest version is from
> Poland: "Even a fly has got a belly,"
> which seems to say that the least among
> us has hunger and aspirations, never
> mind rage.

WHEN THE CATS FALL ASLEEP, THE MOUSE REJOICES AND LEAPS FROM HIS HOLE.
Dum felis dormit, mus gaudet et exsilit antro.

The Roman mouse rejoicing is father to the French mice dancing and English mice playing.

AN ASS AT THE LYRE.
Asinus ad lyram.

A distant relation to the "bull in the china shop."

LIKE BEES AT GEOMETRY.
Ut apes geometriam.

A stinging description of bunglers who've been overwhelmed by their task. Actually, bees do fine in geometry, creating hexagon after hexagon for their honeycombs.

TO HOLD THE WOLF BY THE EARS.
Tenere lupum auribus.

"To beard the lion in his den," or better, "to take the bull by the horns."

WITH CLAWS AND BEAK.
Unguibus et rostro.

"Tooth and nail."

YOU ARE TEACHING A DOLPHIN TO SWIM.
Delphinum natare doces.

> Since we lack a comparable idiom, I
> move we adopt this one.

LATIN IDIOMS ABOUT PROFITS AND MONEY

THE SMELL OF PROFITS IS GOOD WHATEVER IT
COMES FROM.
Lucri bonus odor ex re qualibet.

> *Lucrum,* the Latin word for profit, still
> slinks around in English as "filthy
> lucre." Suetonius tells the story about
> the emperor Vespasian who decided to
> levy a tax on the public urinals of
> Rome. The emperor's son was horrified,
> and said that this was a highly
> undignified way to raise money.
> Vespasian's response was: "Money has
> no smell."

MONEY IS THE QUEEN OF THE WORLD.
Pecunia regina mundi.

> And she makes it go around.

TO GIVE A CAP AND GET A CLOAK.
Pilleum dat ut pallium recipiat.

> To hoodwink someone, or simply to get
> the best of the deal. The French used to

"give an egg to get an ox." In the old English version, you "give a duck to get a goose." The *pilleum*, a small felt skullcap worn at festivals, was ceremoniously given to a slave when he was awarded his freedom. A man still in bondage would have gladly given his cloak to get this cap.

NOTHING STINGS MORE DEEPLY THAN THE LOSS OF MONEY.
Nec quicquam acrius quam pecuniae damnum stimulat.

We don't complain of a sting, but sometimes we're "burned on a deal" or "killed in the market."

THE ABSENT ONE WILL NOT BE THE HEIR.
Absens haeres non erit.

Out of sight, out of the will.

LATIN IDIOMS ABOUT FOOD AND CROCKERY

TO MAKE WAVES IN A CUP.
Exitare fluctus in simpulo.

To create "a tempest in a teapot." (A *simpulum* was a small ladle used for beverages.)

FROM THE EGG TO THE APPLES.
Ab ovo usque ad mala.

> This describes the hors d'oeuvres and the dessert of a Roman dinner party, but it doesn't mean "from soup to nuts," it means "from the beginning to the end."

WE APPLES SWIM.
Nos poma natamus.

> "We are unsinkable." What a grand way for a family, a tribe, or a nation to describe itself.

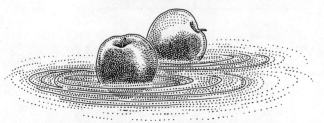

CABBAGE REPEATED.
Crambe repetita.

> This warmed-up, leftover cabbage is comparable to our "chestnut" — a stale joke, a truism. The Greeks put it another way: *Dis krámbe thánatos* (Cabbage, twice over, is death).

A BAD VASE DOESN'T BREAK.
Malum vas non frangitur.

> It's a good line to mutter under your breath as you're sweeping up splinters of Baccarat.

BONES FOR THOSE WHO COME LATE.
Sero venientibus ossa.

> "First come, first served." Or maybe "the early bird catches the worm."

UNBOUGHT FEASTS.
Dapes inemptae.

> An apt description of homegrown produce.

LATIN IDIOMS ABOUT DEEP RIVERS, FAITHLESS REDHEADS, ET CETERA

REDHEADS ARE LESS TRUSTWORTHY.
Rufos esse minus fideles.

> The Romans disliked auburn hair and planted their prejudice all over the empire. At one time, England, France, Spain, and Portugal were all members of the Anti-Redhead League. The antipathy reached its height in Germany: *Rote Haare: Gott bewahre!*

A SCRAPED WRITING TABLET.
Tabula rasa.

> "A clean slate."

SPRING IS NOT ALWAYS GREEN.
Ver non semper viret.

> This has the ring of truth, but I'm not sure what it means. "Youth doesn't always flourish"? "Nothing in this life is certain"? Your guess is better than mine.

WHAT HAS BEEN LOST IS SAFE.
Quae amissa, salva.

> There is small comfort here, but great wisdom.

IT SMELLS OF THE LAMP.
Olet lucernam.

> A sniffy dismissal of a piece of writing that's labored, overwrought. The writer undoubtedly followed another Roman maxim: "Turn the stylus often!" He inverted his stylus and used the blunt end to make so many corrections, revisions, and additions on his wax tablet that the final result reeked of the midnight oil.

THE DEEPEST RIVERS FLOW WITH THE LEAST SOUND.
Altissima quaeque flumina minimo sono labi.

> The Romans — who never stopped talking for a moment — clung to the belief that the man of few words thought fine, deep thoughts. They had another, funnier way of saying it: "Had you been silent, you might have passed

for a philosopher." We believe the same thing, but I don't know why. Still waters so often run shallow.

EVEN LITTLE THINGS HAVE THEIR PECULIAR GRACE.
Inest sua gratia parvis.

We have nothing comparable to this lovely line. "Good things come in small packages" comes to mind, but this usually refers to diminutive people.

WHILE WE LIVE, LET US LIVE.
Dum vivimus, vivamus.

Experts insist that the classical Latin *V* was pronounced as a *W*, but it's hard to accept. Did those glorious orators really say, "Doom wee-wee-moos, wee-wa-moos"? I don't think so and neither does the Catholic Church, for in Ecclesiastical Latin, *V* is *V*. I like to imagine that this old Latin consonant was pronounced as it is in modern Spanish. It's a soft sound, somewhere between a *V* and a *B*, and it's beautiful. *¡Bvaya con Dios!*

A MAN OF THREE LETTERS.
Homo trium literarum.

Not a compliment. The saying alludes to the letters in *fur*, the Latin word for "thief."

LET THE COBBLER STICK TO HIS SANDALS.
Ne sutor ultra crepidam.

We tell the cobbler to stick to his last or
his shoes. According to Pliny, the
phrase was coined by the Roman
painter Apelles, in response to a pushy
shoemaker. The scene plays like
Voltaire: The little cobbler makes his
entrance into the grand studio to give
his opinion of the sandals in a portrait.
The great painter and his apprentices
listen closely as he points out the errors
in the stitching. Flattered by all the
attention, the cobbler goes on and on,
finding fault with the hem of the toga,
the arrangement of lights and darks,
and come to think of it, the nose looks
funny. Apelles begins to frown and
fume, then suddenly explodes,
"Cobbler! Stick to your sandals!"

NOT ANGLES BUT ANGELS.
Non Angli sed angeli.

Angels or not, they were up for sale.
Pope Gregory made the comment as he
glanced at a group of fair-haired British
boys being paraded in front of the
buyers at a Roman slave market.

Latin Sayings: Alive and Well and Living in America

TIME IS USUALLY THE BEST MEDICINE.
Temporis ars medicina fere est.
> The line is by Ovid and he's talking about a cure for the person who is lovesick.

THE DIE IS CAST.
Alea iacta est.
> Die, incidentally, is the singular of dice

NOW OR NEVER.
Nunc aut nunquam.

MANY THINGS SLIP BETWEEN CUP AND LIP.
Multa cadunt inter calicem supremaque labra.

THERE IS A SNAKE CONCEALED IN THE GRASS.
Latet anguis in herba.

THERE'S NO SMOKE WITHOUT FIRE.
Non est fumus absque igne.

HE GIVES TWICE WHO GIVES QUICKLY.
Bis dat qui cito dat.

A ROLLING STONE IS NOT COVERED WITH MOSS.
Saxum volutum non obducitur musco.

WE, TOO, HAVE HURLED JAVELINS.
Et nos quoque tela sparsimus.

> We have so few opportunities to use the wonderful word "javelin" that we hurl it into this saying, accuracy be damned. *(Tela* means "weapons.")

A WORD TO THE WISE IS SUFFICIENT.
Dictum sapienti sat est.

> — Terence

HE WHO WISHES TO AVOID CHARYBDIS FALLS INTO SCYLLA.
Quis vult vitare Charybdim incidit in Scyllam.

> The phrase is familiar, though we're more likely to "jump from the frying pan into the fire." Charybdis was a whirlpool in the Straits of Messina. In an effort to avoid it, sailors often ran aground on the promontory of Scylla. In the *Odyssey,* Homer portrayed Scylla as a lady monster with six heads who plucked six sailors from a ship and devoured them.

HE WHO HAS PROPERTY IN THE SOIL HAS THE SAME UP TO THE SKY.
Cuiuslibet est solum, eius usque ad coelum.

> Though this isn't strictly a proverb, it's a good contemporary definition of air rights.

NO SOONER SAID THAN DONE.
Dictum factum.

THE EXCEPTION PROVES THE RULE.
Exceptio probat regulam.

THE CORRUPTION OF THE BEST IS THE WORST.
Corruptio optimi pessima.

LOVE CONQUERS ALL.
Omnia vincit amor.

— Virgil

THERE IS NO DISPUTING TASTES.
De gustibus non est disputandum.

IGNORANCE OF THE LAW IS NO EXCUSE.
Ignorantia legis neminem excusat.

DON'T TRUST TOO MUCH IN APPEARANCES.
Nimium ne crede colori.

TO THE SICK, WHILE THERE IS LIFE, THERE IS HOPE.
Aegroto dum anima est, spes est.

— Cicero

WILLING AND ABLE.
Volens et potens.

A wry variation of this phrase is the motto of the Earl of Carlisle: *Volo non valeo* (I am willing but unable).

FOREWARNED, FOREARMED.
Praemonitus praemunitus.

FIRST AMONG EQUALS.
Primus inter pares.

LIKE FATHER, LIKE SON.
Qualis pater talis filius.

WHO LOVES ME, LOVES MY DOG.
Qui me amat, amat et canem meam.

"Beware of the dog" was also a sign of
the times.

LATIN THOUGHTS ON WOMEN

**WHAT A WOMAN SAYS TO HER FOND LOVER
SHOULD BE WRITTEN ON AIR OR THE SWIFT WATER.**
Mulier cupido quod dicit amanti,
In vento et rapida scribere oportet aqua.

— Catullus

**WHEN A WOMAN IS OPENLY BAD SHE IS THEN AT HER
BEST.**
Aperte mala cum est mulier, tum demum est bona.

**SHE DANCED MUCH BETTER THAN BECAME A MODEST
WOMAN.**
Saltabat melius quam necesse est probae.

WHEN A WOMAN HAS LOST HER CHASTITY, SHE WILL
SHRINK FROM NO CRIME.
Neque femina amissa pudicitia alia abnuerit.

— Tacitus

PROVIDED A WOMAN BE WELL PRINCIPLED, SHE HAS
DOWRY ENOUGH.
Dummodo morata recte veniat, dotata est satis.

Antipathy toward women was so
prevalent among the ancient Romans
that even a lukewarm commendation is
worth noting. Two cheers, then, for the
old Roman playwright Plautus.

A Few Words from Some Well-Known Romans

MARTIAL
A.D. 40–102. Roman epigrammatist. Born in Spain.

THERE'S NOTHING MORE CONTEMPTIBLE THAN A BALD
MAN WHO PRETENDS TO HAVE HAIR.
Calvo turpius est nihil compto.

WHOEVER IS NOT TOO WISE IS WISE.
Quisquis plus justo non sapit, ille sapit.

IF FAME COMES AFTER DEATH, I'M IN NO HURRY FOR IT.
Si post fata venit gloria non propero.

I DO NOT LOVE YOU, ZABIDI, I CANNOT TELL YOU WHY,
BUT THIS I KNOW, I DO NOT LOVE YOU, ZABIDI.
Non amo te Zabidi, nec possum dicere quare,
Hoc solum scio, non amo te, Zabidi.

> The seventeeth-century English version
> of this couplet ("I do not love thee,
> Doctor Fell, the reason why I cannot
> tell . . .") is almost as well known as the
> original. Parody, however, doesn't
> diminish the power of Martial's words.
> It's the terrible gentleness of the
> rejection that haunts us.

JUVENAL
  Circa A.D. 60–140. Roman satirical poet.

DARE TO DO SOMETHING WORTHY OF EXILE AND PRISON
IF YOU MEAN TO BE ANYBODY. VIRTUE IS PRAISED AND
LEFT TO FREEZE.
Aude aliquid brevibus Gyaris et carcere dignum
Si vis esse aliquis. Probitas laudatur et alget.

OF WHAT ADVANTAGE IS IT TO YOU, PONTICUS, TO
QUOTE YOUR REMOTE ANCESTORS AND TO EXHIBIT THEIR
PORTRAITS?
Quid prodest, Pontice, longo
Sanguine censeri pictosque ostendere vultus majorum?

NOBODY EVER BECAME DEPRAVED ALL AT ONCE.
Nemo repente fuit turpissimus.

PERSIUS
   A.D. 34–62. Roman Stoic satirist.

RETIRE WITHIN YOURSELF, AND YOU WILL DISCOVER
HOW SMALL A STOCK THERE IS.
Tecum habita, et noris quam sit tibi curta supellex.

> A friend of mine was once trapped by
> himself in an elevator for five hours.
> When he emerged he said, "I just
> discovered I've only got four hours'
> worth of personal resources."

CICERO
   106–43 B.C. Roman orator, statesman, and prose writer.

THERE IS NOTHING SO ABSURD AS NOT TO HAVE BEEN
SAID BY A PHILOSOPHER.
Nihil tam absurdum, quod non dictum sit ab aliquo philosophorum.

CAN ANYONE FIND OUT IN WHAT CONDITION HIS BODY
WILL BE, I DO NOT SAY A YEAR HENCE, BUT THIS
EVENING?
*An id exploratum cuiquam potest esse, quomodo sese habiturum sit
corpus, non dico ad annum sed ad vesperam?*

TACITUS
   Circa A.D. 54–118. Roman historian.

IT IS HUMAN NATURE TO HATE THOSE WHOM WE HAVE
INJURED.
Proprium humani ingenii est, odisse quem laeseris.

OVID
43 B.C.–A.D. 17. Roman poet.

LOVERS REMEMBER EVERYTHING.
Meminerunt omnia amantes.

IF HE DID NOT SUCCEED, HE AT LEAST FAILED IN A GLORIOUS
UNDERTAKING.
Quem si non tenuit magnis tamen excidit ausis.

FOR THIS REASON, IF YOU BELIEVE IN PROVERBS
LET ME TELL YOU THE COMMON ONE:
"IT IS UNLUCKY TO MARRY IN MAY."
Hac quoque de causa, si te proverbia tangunt,
Mense malos Maio nubere vulgus ait.

WE ARE CHARMED BY NEATNESS: LET NOT YOUR HAIR BE
OUT OF ORDER.
Munditiis capimur: non sine lege capilli.

THERE IS NO SMALL PLEASURE IN PURE WATER.
Est in aqua dulci non invidiosa voluptas.

IT IS ART TO CONCEAL ART.
Ars est celare artem.

I SEE AND APPROVE BETTER THINGS,
I FOLLOW THE WORSE.
Video meliora proboque,
Deteriora sequor.

PUBLILIUS SYRUS
Flourished 45 B.C. Roman writer.

A BEAUTIFUL FACE IS A SILENT RECOMMENDATION.
Formosa facies muta commendatio est.

> The same thought occurred to Ovid: "A pleasing face is no small advantage." And to Virgil: "Even virtue is fairer when it appears in a beautiful person." The best version of all is anonymous: *Sat pulchra, si sat bona* (Handsome enough is good enough).

IT IS A KINDNESS TO IMMEDIATELY REFUSE WHAT YOU INTEND TO DENY.
Pars beneficii est, quod petitur, si cito neges.

VIRGIL
70–19 B.C. Roman poet.

THEY CAN, WHO THINK THEY CAN.
Possunt, quia posse videntur.

GO ON AND INCREASE IN VALOR, MY BOY, THIS IS THE WAY TO THE STARS.
Macte nova virtute, puer,
Sic itur ad astra.

> "To reach the stars" means to achieve immortality.

PLAUTUS
Circa 254–184 B.C. Roman comic dramatist.

THERE IS NOTHING MORE FRIENDLY THAN A FRIEND IN
NEED.
Nihil homini amico est opportuno amicius.

TATTLETALES, AND THOSE WHO LISTEN TO THEIR
SLANDER, BY MY GOOD WILL, SHOULD ALL BE HANGED.
THE FORMER BY THEIR TONGUES, THE LATTER BY THEIR
EARS.
*Homines qui gestant, quique auscultant crimina, si meo arbitratu
liceat, omnes pendeant gestores linguis, auditores auribus.*

IT'S A WRETCHED BUSINESS
TO BE DIGGING A WELL
JUST AS THIRST IS OVERCOMING YOU.
Miserum est opus,
Igitur demum fodere puteum,
Ubi sitis fauces tenet.

PLINY THE ELDER
A.D. 23–79. Roman naturalist, counselor to emperors. He
died in the eruption of Vesuvius.

THERE IS ALWAYS SOMETHING NEW OUT OF AFRICA.
Ex Africa semper aliquid novi.

> He's paraphrasing Aristotle's words:
> "There is always something new out of
> Libya."

AUGUSTUS CAESAR
63 B.C.–A.D. 14. Roman emperor.

HASTEN SLOWLY.
Festina lente.

TERENCE
Circa 190–158 B.C. Roman comic dramatist. Born in North Africa; brought to Rome as a slave.

DO NOT DO WHAT IS ALREADY DONE.
Actum ne agas.

SENECA
Circa A.D. 1–66. Roman philosopher, poet, dramatist, statesman. Born in Spain.

NOTHING COSTS SO MUCH AS WHAT IS BOUGHT BY PRAYERS.
Nulla res carius constat quam quae precibus empta est.

THE PART OF LIFE WE REALLY LIVE IS SHORT.
Exigua pars est vitae quam nos vivimus.

A MULTITUDE OF BOOKS DISTRACTS THE MIND.
Distrahit animum librorum multitudo.

CATULLUS
Circa 85–54 B.C. Roman lyric poet.

NOTHING IS SILLIER THAN A SILLY LAUGH.
Risu inepto res ineptior nulla est.

About the Author

Suzanne Brock was born in Colorado, grew up in California, and worked for many years as a journalist and advertising writer in New York City. She now divides her time between Shelter Island, New York, and Marbella, in the south of Spain. Her hobby in both places is gardening.